God Uses CROOKED STICKS

Our family's 30+ year adventure of serving & learning

With Jesus in Africa

Me with one of the first Sunday schools, 1981

God Uses Crooked Sticks

Our family's 30+ year adventure of serving & learning
with Jesus in Africa

Lorella Rouster

Every Child Ministries

2017

First Printing: 2017

ISBN: 978-1-387-01315-9

Every Child Ministries
PO Box 810
Hebron, IN 46341

www.ecmafrica.org

Author's personal website : www.lovecongo.org

Ordering Information:

Special discounts are available on quantity purchases by corporations, associations, educators, and others. For details, contact the publisher at the above listed address.

U.S. trade bookstores and wholesalers: Please contact Every Child Ministries Tel: (219) 996-4201; Fax: (219) 996-4203; or email : lrouster@ecmafrica.org.

DEDICATION

*To my husband John, my greatest encourager
and No. 1 partner in this great adventure--*

*Thank you, honey. Without your constant support,
patience, and love for the Lord,
this adventure would never have been realized.*

TABLE OF CONTENTS

ACKNOWLEDGEMENTS

I would like thank my beloved husband John for allowing me to tap into his astounding ability for remembering historical details and my good friends Margie Jackson and Monica Miles for their sharp eyes and editorial expertise.

I also realize that I may never have become motivated to become a Bible teacher had I not first seen that modeled in a highly attractive way by Rev. Francis (Uncle Fran the Bible Man) Goodman of Rural Bible Mission. It was under his ministry that I first heard the Gospel that I eventually came to cherish. Thank you, Uncle Fran!

Thank you also to Billy Walker, the evangelist who pressed the Gospel home to me as a teenager and under whose ministry I came to Christ, and to Cheryl Philippi, who invited me to those special meetings at Michigan Center Bible Church. You turned my life around!

Thank you to Pastor Bill Enslen, under whose ministry John came to salvation, and Richard Howard, who accompanied him to our home one night and shared the Gospel. I can never thank you enough!

Finally, thank you to our beloved children, Carrie, Sharon, John Henry, Kristi, and Whitney who we raised as a daughter. We are thrilled that you were a part of our journey and humbled and grateful that knowing our faults as you do, you still support our ministry.

APOLOGY

The term "Crooked Sticks" comes from a saying attributed to a Mennonite missionary to Congo* named Archie Graber. He said, "I don't know why the Lord chooses like He does; but if He can use a crooked stick like me, He can use anybody." Our family often referred to this quote as we reported to our supporting churches, sometimes showing a very crooked walking stick my husband John made from the roots of bushes dug out of the mission airstrip at Garizim, Congo. It always reminded us of our multitudinous shortcomings, and yet encouraged us that in spite of it all, God was willing and able to use us as a part of His eternal purposes.

(From War to be One by Levi Keidel, p. 239, Zondervan, c 1977)

INTRODUCTION

I have always hated it when I hear missionaries say something like, "We thought we were going to Timbuktu to share the Gospel with the unreached, but looking back we realize it was really all about God teaching us."

My heart would always rebel at those explanations. "What?" I would think. "People spent thousands of dollars and you spent your life just so you could learn to be more thankful? Why did Jesus give the Great Commission, then? It doesn't sound to me like it was about teaching you, but rather about reaching the lost."

Now, with thirty-plus years of African ministry behind us, I have come to peace with this. I realize now that it doesn't have to be an either-or proposition. I still believe the reason God calls missionaries is to reach the lost, and doing so has been our greatest joy and most enduring reward. But along the way, we missionaries have a lot to learn, too. We are all crooked sticks—sinners, the Bible calls us. And our wonderful, amazing God uses us for His eternal purposes at the same time He is teaching us and honing us for greater service. It's been our privilege and joy to be Crooked Sticks in His hand.

Joyfully in His Service,

Lorella Rouster

God Uses Crooked Sticks

KEEPING IT ALL STRAIGHT
(Times and Places)

These memories are written topically, not chronologically, meaning our circumstances may seem to move back and forth. First, we may be in a mud hut, then in a cement house, then in a mud hut again. To help you orient the stories, here is a simple timeline:

1979-1980 God called us, we sold our farm in Indiana, we prepared for service and built our support team.

1981-1984 Our family's first term at Mission Nkara, in Congo working with Jim and Nancy Smith and family. At the time, all of us were working with AMG International. The Smiths later founded Laban Ministries. We lived in a cement house, with electricity in the evening by generator. During this time, we adopted baby Kristi. I taught at Ecole Biblique Laban, started the first Sunday schools with Bible school students, and began developing the basics of what eventually became ECM's Teacher Training manual.

1984-1985 Living in Cedar Lake, IN, we helped start Every Child Ministries (ECM) with some Christian friends. Incorporation was confirmed on December 4, 1985.

1985-1989 Still living at Cedar Lake, I led a six-week summer trip every year, the teams and I traveling (hitchhiking, mostly) all around Kinshasa and Bandundu Province with teacher training seminars. John worked to support the family and we worked as volunteers developing Every Child Ministries and my Teacher Training Manual in Kituba. Our daughters Carrie and Sharon both helped with summer seminar ministry. John Henry completed high school and Kristi was in elementary school.

1990-1996 Second term in Congo, served at Mission Garizim. We lived in a mud hut, no electricity in the hut. Eventually we installed solar power for electricity at the training center. Our son John Henry served with us for nine months before going in the Army, and Kristi was also with us. Floyd Bertsch served as International Director in the States.

1997 John and I became International Directors for ECM. Kristi's daughter Whitney was born.

1999 ECM entered Ghana.

> 2001 Began public school ministry in Ghana with the program, "Character Building from the Bible." Led many teaching teams with that program in following years. Also began ministry to street children in downtown Accra.

> 2002 Haven of Hope Children's Home was built and opened in Ghana.

> 2003 First liberation of shrine slaves was held in Ghana.

2005 Teacher Training Seminars in Togo and Benin, resulting in a small but long-term presence in Benin

2006 ECM entered Uganda, adopting the Tegot Atoo IDP camp as our first project. Soon after, the first albino project was started.

2015 Mark Luckey became International Director.

2016 On August 30, John officially retired, continuing to serve ECM as a volunteer. I served as an advisor to projects involving fighting child trafficking.

2017 I moved into missionary status, serving Congolese children and families by writing Bible lessons for children in the African Kituba language and traveling to Africa two to three times a year to train national leaders. I take a special interest in bringing the Gospel to devotees of African traditional religion.

God Uses Crooked Sticks

CHAPTER 1
Learning to hear God's voice –
The adventure begins!

As my husband John drove up I-69 he seemed unusually quiet and preoccupied. Our three children had been spending a few days with their grandparents, and we were going to pick them up. I tried several different topics of conversation, but John remained silent. "What's the matter? Don't you feel well?" I finally asked. John began sobbing. Now he had my attention. In the twelve years of our marriage, I had never before seen him shed a tear. Was this my husband sobbing? Then I was quiet, waiting.

Finally, he spoke. "I...just...think...God is calling us to be missionaries and go to Africa!" He choked out the words and continued sobbing.

It was Palm Sunday, 1980. John had always been extremely, exuberantly happy fulfilling his lifelong dream of owning his own dairy farm. He loved working with his Registered Holstein cattle and never even thought of doing anything else.

I had gone back to college when our youngest, John Henry, began kindergarten. I had completed my teaching degree, and was teaching English and journalism at a nearby high school, doing freelance writing on the side.

I loved teaching, and I loved writing, but I never forgot that I had been called to be a missionary. I had made some poor choices as a young adult, one thing had led to another, and it seemed I would never be able to fulfill that calling. I was a useless stick that God could not use, I thought. At least not in my original calling.

Yet that calling seemed to grow. When I read missionary biographies or heard missionaries speak, the drawing inside myself was almost unbearable. In the early days of my teaching career, I had shared my personal dilemma with Christian friends who had a campus ministry at the school. We began to pray about it together weekly. I had been praying, "Lord, either take this burden away from me, or give it to John."

I never talked about it with him, though. I knew such a thing was unthinkable. John was too happy farming.

When John got his sobbing under control, he told me that he had had an unusual experience that morning. He was just enjoying milking his cows, as he always did, when suddenly it was just as if Jesus was standing right beside him, saying, "I want you to go to Africa as a missionary."

When I heard that, I barely restrained myself from jumping through the roof shouting, "Hallelujah!" From that moment on, our family's life was never the same again. We knew we had heard God's voice, and a thirty-plus-year adventure had begun.

Our letters crossed in the mail

I am a teacher at heart, so I looked forward to homeschooling our three children while we were in Congo, and was willing to pitch in and do what I could to help teach the other missionary kids, too. I also looked forward to lots of ministry in the villages and Bible school, and soon got heavily involved. It wasn't long before I realized that I could really use help, especially with our son John Henry. He was super-intelligent at practical problem-solving but did not really enjoy book learning. As I discussed this with my husband John, he thought of a young lady we had met recently at one of our supporting churches. She was from a similar background as ours, and we had connected well. "Why don't you write and ask Cindy Hawkins if she'd be interested," he said. Immediately, I felt a sense of peace about that idea, so I wrote inviting Cindy to consider coming out and helping. We offered to let her live with us. The next time an MAF (Mission Aviation Fellowship) plane arrived, we sent the letter.

After a short time, we got a letter from Cindy. It was evident that she had not yet received our letter, but she was asking if she could come, and suggesting that she might help with the kids' schooling. God had planted the idea in her mind at the same time He had put it in ours, and our letters had crossed in the mail.

Cindy did come out, and she was such a great blessing. Not only did she help with John Henry's schooling, but she was a great companion to our girls, Carrie and

Sharon. With her help, I was able to commit more time to the growing Sunday school work. Cindy traveled with us to many villages and became like another daughter to us. We have maintained a close friendship ever since, and we always remember how clearly God spoke in bringing her to us.

CHAPTER 2
Learning to live simply and creatively

Our introduction to Congo

Our introduction to Congo showed us right away that we should prepare our minds to live simply. While we were raising our support, we decided that John and I should leave our three children with friends for a couple of weeks and take a short trip together to see what we were getting into. We did that in January 1981. Jim Smith, the missionary we would be working with, met us at Njili Airport in Kinshasa. It was pouring rain and the air was steamy like a hot shower. The window by the driver's seat in Jim's vehicle had been broken out, and it was covered with a sheet of plastic, duct-taped on and flapping in the wind. The windshield wipers were also broken, so that as he drove, Jim had to reach his arm out through the flapping plastic and work the windshield wiper by hand. We immediately knew we had arrived on the other side of the world.

As we drove out to Ecole Biblique (Bible School) Laban where we would be living and working with the Jim and Nancy Smith family at Nkara, we passed thousands of simple, grass-roofed huts. Most were made by pounding sharpened sticks into the ground, lacing them together with a tough vine I later learned was called *nkodi*, and packing the walls with mud. The floors were just packed mud. We saw hundreds of women out in their yards, pounding manioc roots to powder in a tub-sized mortar and pestle arrangement called a *kibuka*, made from a hollowed-out log. We crossed over bridges made of rickety planks and over sandy and muddy roads filled with deep ruts like we had never seen before.

We were only in Congo two weeks, and we had debated whether it was worth the investment for that short time. However, after we returned with our own pictures and stories, it seemed like everyone took us much more seriously. We were no longer a farmer and an English teacher chasing wild dreams. We were serious missionaries.

By June we had raised our support with some input from the sale of our farm, sold most of our personal possessions, and packed what we thought would be useful. We returned with our three children—Carrie, then 13; Sharon, 11; and John Henry, 9. When we arrived, Jim was not there to meet us, but we soon saw a sign saying ROUSTERS. We met Ted and Betty Berklund, who ordered supplies for the missionaries, and who quickly became our first missionary friends. They explained that Jim had received two telegrams. One named the flight on which we were arriving. The other said we were having visa problems and could not come until they were solved. Both telegrams arrived the same day, and neither was dated! So which was sent first? A trip to Kinshasa from the interior is expensive and time-consuming, so Jim sent Burklunds to check it out and let him know whether we had arrived. They took us to a missionary guest house, where we waited a week for Jim to come. We didn't yet have a vehicle, so every day we took walks around Kinshasa. Finally, Jim met us and we were glad to be on our way to the interior at last.

When we came to the bottom of the deep valley on the *Mai Ndombe* (Black Water) River, we stopped at a wooded area. Jim pointed into the woods to the right. "The boys' bathroom is over there," he said, and to the left, "The girls' is over there." It took me just a minute to get his meaning. For the first of many, many times, we girls went to the left to squat in the beautiful woods. As we came to the water's edge, a swarm of beautiful blue butterflies flitted up into the air. It seemed like God's seal of approval on our simple bathroom facilities and our new journey in life.

At a town named Kenge along the way, someone noticed that gas was slowly leaking from the vehicle. John knew how to temporarily repair fine cracks by rubbing bar soap into them. This simple fix enabled us to go on until we got to the town of Kikwit where we met Jim's mechanic Ngundu. There, the engine broke down entirely. Eventually, a Mennonite missionary from Kikwit towed us into town and later took us out to the Mission station at Nkara where the Smith family served.

On both trips, from the time we disembarked from the Sabena (Belgian) Airlines plane, until we made it out to Nkara, virtually everything we saw and everything that happened to us shouted that we should be preparing ourselves to live simply.

Easing into a simpler life

Fortunately, God eased us into that, providing a cement house for us our first term. It wasn't until our second term at *Mission Garizim* that He asked us to live in a mud and thatch house. Our first term, the mission had a generator that we ran in the evenings or whenever electricity was needed. It was not until our second term that we lived without electricity in our home. In both places, we paid workers to carry water for us from nearby springs, which we stored in 50 gallon barrels. Our first term, we only had to accustom ourselves to bailing a bucket of water out of the barrel to flush the toilet. Our second term we dug a hole in the ground and made an old-fashioned outhouse.

Despite the simple lifestyle, we found Africa a great place to raise kids. Their lives were varied, interesting, and constructive. Carrie and Sharon learned to make marshmallows from scratch, and to sew fancy quilts by hand. They enjoyed "*diotos*," kid-sized potlucks to which friends brought baby birds cooked in a sauce (not so much fun). Each of the girls had a special friend amongst the women teachers at the local school. Carrie's friend was called Jolina, and Sharon's was Lina. There was swimming every day, homemade skits with the Smith kids—Shawn, Nicol, Todd and Jack, an introduction to the piano from Nancy Smith, and family hymn singing with the Smiths every Sunday night.

Sharon learned to crochet, a skill she has enjoyed ever since, and Carrie got to introduce children to crayons for the first time as a VBS teacher (more about that later). Both the girls got to help deliver babies, including some problematic births, and help in many ways at our local dispensary, including emergency trips to help someone in distress in the middle of the night. They also helped teach women to read Kituba in a literacy class. Carrie and I got out our clarinets and Sharon her flute, and we played "It Is Well with My Soul" in the local church service. John Henry learned to kill bats with his BB gun, make huts, eat Congolese food, and speak Kituba like a native. It was a rich, full life.

Celebrating our fiftieth anniversary in 2017. What an adventure we've enjoyed together!

CHAPTER 3
Learning how God had prepared us

Farming as missionary preparation

As we got into Congolese life, we found that God had prepared us for this time in many ways. John often found that his experience with cows served him well. Pinkeye was a common malady around the villages, and many people were coming to our missionary friends complaining of this bothersome infection. John remembered that his cows had sometimes got pinkeye, and that the vet had put a drop of penicillin in their eyes. He had brought some penicillin with him as a general precaution, because we knew that little was available locally. John tried putting drops in one person's eyes. The recovery was remarkable, and word spread quickly. Every morning the line of people seeking treatment for pinkeye grew. Fortunately, no one had a reaction to the penicillin, and every person got better. Finally, the line began to diminish, and we were thankful that we had been able to help so many.

Working in my local church as missionary preparation

I had loved teaching the Bible to children in the States and had done everything from Sunday school to Vacation Bible School, to children's clubs in homes and local parks, to serving on a Christian education committee at my church and writing Bible lessons both for my local church and for publication. I had taught fifth and sixth grade girls for eight years at my church. During that time I had worked my way through much of the Old Testament, greatly enhancing my overall understanding of the historical flow and great themes of Scripture. I had also developed some active teaching methods, discovering how much my girls enjoyed acting out Bible stories.

In Congo (it was called Zaire when we lived there, but I'll call it by its present name, Congo), I was asked to teach a Christian education class at Ecole Biblique Laban. It was pretty basic at first, because I was working on learning the Kituba language at the same time, while teaching missionary kids in the morning – both ours and the Smiths. Yet out of that class grew the training program that eventually became the core of Every Child Ministries, the mission organization we helped to start during our second term.

The first Sunday school was begun at Nkara with me teaching. Word had spread of this new venture, and people came from other villages—early. I was still in my robe, sipping coffee and relaxing, when the Smiths' daughter Nicol came running over to our house. "Aunt Lorella!" she said, "the church is already full of kids waiting for Sunday school to start." It was still a full hour until Sunday school was supposed to begin, but I dressed quickly and hurried down the hill to the church to meet the kids. I had only been in Congo three months, so I had spent about 15 hours that week, after the lesson had been prepared in English, translating it into Kituba, and that with a lot of help. Although I despise teachers reading their lessons, I have to admit that that's pretty much what I did that first Sunday. It was all I really could do. Afterwards, I asked some girls if they had understood. They seemed hesitant. "Well, a little," they finally answered.

God Uses Crooked Sticks

I soon turned the Nkara Sunday school over to one of the Bible school students I had been training, and began a new school in another village, and then another, and then another. By the end of our first term in 1983, there were 16 Sunday schools in local villages, mostly taught by Bible school students. I had also learned to speak Kituba so that people could understand me, and without translating from English. I had begun with the firm foundation I had gained working in the U.S. as a volunteer with Child Evangelism Fellowship, and had tried adapting teaching methods to Congolese culture in various ways. God used that to enable us to continue helping African churches learn to reach children. As this book is published in 2017, there are over 3,200 Sunday schools established through training given with the methods we began to develop there at Nkara.

During our second term, at Garizim, I led our students in trying out a more thoroughly active method of teaching. I called it "Malembe-malembe" or "Step-by-Step." In it, we taught the Bible in a thorough, systematic manner, verse by verse, much like expository preaching through a book. However, instead of telling students what happened, we divided up the passage into very small parts. Then we read or had them read one part—one to three verses. This was followed by asking questions to which they responded, then acting out what happened in that short section, and finally singing and dancing what happened in that section. We tried it first with the story of Jonah, teaching those four chapters of the Bible in 16 lessons. It was very popular, and we used the Step-by-Step method later to teach Genesis and other passages.

Having African teachers and students act out Bible stories was often quite interesting. They were so uninhibited! I remember Mama Kongolo, one of our teachers, pretending she was the donkey bringing Jesus into Jerusalem while students cheered and waved flowers, and one "rode" her.

In the story of the son who wasted his inheritance, children pretended to be pigs, crawling around and making appropriate noises. In a Christmas play, a star was rigged on a string so that it moved as the "wise men" followed it, and Herod's soldiers came marching in, wearing sunglasses hand carved from *mikobodi*, a soft African wood, and carrying fake wooden guns over their shoulders, looking for the baby Jesus to destroy Him.

One of my favorite examples of African realism came years later in Ghana. We had started a children's home and school there, and Comfort, about seven years old, was playing Mary in a Christmas pageant. She came in with Joseph and looked very, very pregnant with a huge pillow stuffed in her shirt. Suddenly she stopped and cried out, "Help me, Joseph! The baby is coming!" A curtain was quickly put up by other students, and in a few moments, we saw Mary (now with flat tummy), Joseph, and the baby Jesus. I laughed and laughed at their innocent realism, and I doubt that anyone who saw it will ever forget the Christmas story as they presented it.

As I remember these scenes from Africa, I remember when I was teaching in my local church years before, and decided to have my girls try to act out the children of Israel crossing the Jordan River. A simple experimentation in America— now become full-blown in Africa. Thank you, Lord, for preparing me in even these simple matters to serve you in Africa.

God Uses Crooked Sticks

A painful childhood as missionary preparation

God had also prepared me for this through hard experiences. As a child, I was painfully shy and introverted. I always dreamed of being well-liked and popular. The only problem was, I had absolutely no idea how to talk to my peers, and even less confidence to do so. Throughout all my school years up until I turned to Christ late in my sophomore year, I can honestly say that I do not remember speaking a single word to anyone, nor did any of my classmates ever talk to me. I went to many school and public dances and sat by myself, watching others whirl around the floor. I joined clubs, but I never interacted with anyone. I did not know how. During my junior high years in particular, I felt brutally alone.

Later, when I came to Christ, I took my focus off myself and it gradually became easier to talk to others. As a result, I have been privileged to have a few close friends. In my African experience, I found that God used my years of painful loneliness to help me empathize with children who are marginalized or outcast. I always gravitate to the underdog, feeling the pain of those who are put down by others. It is probably the reason why, years later, I chose the tagline "Hope for the forgotten children of Africa" to describe the heart of Every Child Ministries.

At the same time, I have learned over the years to entertain myself. After I became a Christian and began to experience God's love and acceptance, I learned to enjoy spending time alone, even as I grew in my ability to interact with others. I needed both of those abilities as a missionary. Raising and maintaining support as a missionary required constant interaction with people, and that stretched me greatly. On the other hand, my evenings alone in Africa were many while John was in Kikwit or Kinshasa procuring supplies. Those evenings were often without light, or at least, not light that was sufficient for reading. Because I had learned to be content alone and to entertain myself, I was able to thrive under both circumstances, and eventually even to thank God for the painful, lonely years. They were years of preparation.

Things my Daddy taught me as missionary preparation

My upbringing was perhaps a bit unusual. Our family was poor, although I did not know it until much later and never felt poor. To say that we worked hard is an understatement. There were the usual household tasks of that time—family ironing every Saturday, weeding our large family garden, shelling beans and peas, canning hundreds of quarts of vegetables every year, cleaning, and mowing the yard with an old-fashioned hand-powered push mower. My favorite job was sprinkling the flowers and garden. We didn't have a sprinkler nozzle, so I partially blocked the hose with my thumb to create a sprinkling effect.

There were also other jobs that I never heard of other kids doing. My dad was a welder who did odd jobs making things for people in his spare time. His shop was his paradise. He used to bring home boxes of nuts, bolts and washers that his shop was discarding. Several nights a week, my job was to sort them into empty jars my mom saved for him. I disliked the job because it was greasy and dirty and hard on my fingernails. It was also endless, so there was never the sense of satisfaction that comes from completing a job. He also brought home fifty-gallon drums filled with metal shavings—brass and iron mixed together. My job was to put a few shovels full at a time into a plastic bucket and to use a large magnet to pull out all the iron. I had to pull it off the magnet into another bucket and keep doing so until the brass and iron were completely separated so that my dad could sell them both for scrap metal. That also was an endless job.

When I wanted a bicycle, my dad made one for me from scrap parts, but I had to participate. My job was to sand the rusty framework until it shone. Over and over, my dad would come to inspect my work and send me back to work to sand off a fleck of rust here and another there. I learned to persevere, and I learned the satisfaction of a job well done.

The most unusual job I had as a child was helping to dig a basement under our home. It was a family project that lasted several years. At first there was only a small crawl space under the house. My dad decided to dig a basement to provide storage space for the veggies we canned every year. Dad broke up the ground of the crawl space with a pick. My mom shoveled the loose dirt into a bucket. My brother and I took turns, one of us hoisting the filled bucket up to the small window of the crawl space, and the other putting it into our wagon. When the wagon was full, we pulled it to low spots in the yard and dumped it. Later we had to rake the dirt around to even it out. Bit by bit the basement grew, my dad and mom propping up the house with jacks and beams and eventually pouring cement walls.

I hated those jobs, yet when I got to Africa, I realized they had prepared me to work hard, to accept distasteful tasks as part of life, and to keep working over a long time even in unpleasant circumstances. Had I not learned those values as a child, I do not believe I could have endured as a missionary in the interior of Congo, which was still quite primitive and very often uncomfortable. Because of the way I grew up, I did not expect life to be easy. I enjoyed comfort, but I didn't expect it. Yes, I was well prepared for Congo. Thank you, Daddy!

In addition, after years of jobs that I hated, it seems like such a privilege to me now to be able to do work I love. Most of the time, my work seems much more enjoyable than any recreation I can think of. Thank you, Daddy!

CHAPTER 4
Learning to embrace discomfort

Living in the interior of Congo—in the "bush" as it was commonly called, gave us many opportunities to embrace – well, let's not call it *hardship;* let's call it *discomfort* – for the sake of the Gospel. My husband John and I had both grown up in poor families that worked hard, and I had read scores of missionary biographies, so we went to Congo expecting to experience some discomfort. We learned to laugh at each new uncomfortable circumstance, saying, "This will make a great newsletter."

Learning to live with termites

Termites were a source of discomfort several times. My first experience with termites came during our first term at Nkara. I took turns with others helping out in a bookstore. On a corner shelf, there was one set of books that we did not sell often. One day a buyer came for some of those books. I reached out to take some books from the stack, and poof! The whole stack, about a foot high, disintegrated into a small pile of dust on the shelf. Termites had come through the wood shelf and had eaten all the books, carefully leaving only a very thin outer shell so that it looked like the stack was still there.

During the late 1980's, we were living in the U.S. and I was spending about six weeks in Congo every summer leading a training team. My next experience with termites was on one of those trips. The church had set up a bed for me in one of their offices that had a thin cement floor. The cement had small cracks in it, and during the night, termites came up through a crack and got into a canvas suitcase filled with materials I had prepared for the Sunday schools. When I opened it the next day, it was filled with confetti—and a few termites that must have grown too fat to get out again. The only thing I could do was to haul it out to the chickens. Boy, did they have a feast that day!

When we moved to Garizim in 1990, we had many experiences with termites. I should have learned from my experience with the Sunday school supplies, but when we finally arrived at our mud hut home after a very long day of hard travel, there were not many options. We had brought our personal items in suitcases. Everything else was to follow later in a sea container. We were using 3x5 diskettes for our computer in those days, and I was concerned that the container might be too hot for them. To protect our data, I had brought it on diskettes in our suitcases. There was a bed in the mud hut home, but no other furniture as yet, so we set our suitcases on logs to keep them off the bare dirt floor. In the morning, we found that termites had not only invaded our suitcases, but also eaten holes in our clothes and destroyed all our computer diskettes. At least our clothing had not been turned into confetti!

Everything about termites is not destructive, however. John cooked our first few meals at *Mission Garizim* over a campfire while we were waiting for the arrival of the wood-burning cook stove which later arrived from Nkara where we had previously served. The Congolese told us they could teach us to make an oven out of a termite hill. There was a big mound near our hut, about seven feet high. I watched them as they made the oven. First, they cut an opening in the side of the mound at ground level. Then they dug in until they found a huge egg-shaped piece of earth made of a different color and quality of soil. This was the queen's chamber, they informed me. They dug that out, and found the queen—an ugly creature about six inches long, with a tiny head and a huge, fat body about two inches in diameter. Her skin was translucent and you could see oily fat squishing around just under her skin. They offered her to me because they said only women could eat her. When I turned down that delicacy, they seemed delighted that they would be able to take a treat home to their wives.

Once the queen's chamber was cleared, the worker termites fled, running all over the feet of our Congolese helpers in their hurry to exit. There was already an air passage to the top of the mound, so the workers built a fire inside the mound until it was very hot. Then they pulled the fire out, put our bread dough in on a scrap piece of metal, and put another piece of metal over the opening. Twenty minutes or so later, out popped nice fresh bread, with only a few pieces of fallen soil on it to remind us where it had been baked. We used the termite hill oven for several months until our wood cook stove arrived.

We also collected anthills, similar to the termite mounds, since the soil has special qualities that make it a good substitute for asphalt, being mixed with the saliva of ants or termites. Missionary Erik Carlson, who worked with us for a year along with his wife, Bambi, built an airstrip which was later finished by my husband John, using this pulverized soil.

However, termites usually brought us discomfort. They were attracted to soft materials. Soft paper attached to walls was eaten quickly, but hard, polished paper was refused. We set the legs of our dining table in small cans filled with kerosene so that the termites could not crawl up them to eat our table. However, the critters seemed to know whether we were home or not home. Every time we left for a few days, they would build a column underneath the wooden table, until they would actually reach the table and begin feasting on it from the underside. They regularly ate the thatch roof of our hut and outside toilet, so that it had to be repaired and even replaced often. When we would go outside at night, we could hear a whirring sound "Whooom! Whooom!" and see termites beating their hind legs on the thatch. We never figured out exactly what they were doing. We were fortunate that after that first night, we never again had major losses to termites, even though we lived in that mud hut for six years. I guess we finally learned how to co-exist.

Learning to live with critters

Our mud hut home at Garizim was also an attraction to rats. We placed D-Con around to kill them, but sometimes it took time to work. One day I was sick in bed with malaria. I was lying under a mosquito net, passing the time by reading a light novel that did not require much concentration. In front of the bed was a shelf built from sticks lashed together with the tough native vine called *nkodi* that was used for building native huts. On the shelf were our suitcases with our clothing arranged in them, and a big carton of toilet paper. We bought such supplies in quantity because we got into town only about once every three or four months.

God Uses Crooked Sticks

As I looked at the carton of toilet paper, I noticed that the paper was unrolling and coming out of the carton. My eyes followed it as it disappeared under my bed. I rolled over and looked on the other side of the bed. It was coming out from under the bed and going down a hole in the dirt floor of our hut-home. Rats were using it to build an underground nest! I broke off the paper and watched the end disappear down the hole. I half expected that in a few minutes, a rat would poke its head out of the hole looking for more, but that did not happen. It's a good thing I was there that day, or we might have wondered how we went through all our toilet paper so fast!

I like my experience with rats better than my husband's. John was in bed with malaria one day, napping. When he woke up, he was looking right into the face of a rat perched on top on his mosquito net, peering down into its face.

We found that rats were attracted to shiny things even in the dark. I had a couple of scarves that had some shiny metallic threads woven into them. We found those scarves woven through the thatch roof of our bedroom, where we guessed rats had unsuccessfully tried to pull them into their nest, and we never were able to untangle them from the roof without tearing the scarves to shreds.

Driver ants were another source of real discomfort for us. At first it was just getting a few up the leg by inadvertently stepping on a stream of them passing over the path. Even one could cause considerable discomfort, for their pincers were very sharp and clung tightly. A few times we stepped on the edge of a stream of ants and spent considerable time picking them out of our thongs, where they kept pinching tightly to the foam.

My worst experience with driver ants came one night at
Mission Garizim. I got up in the night to use the outdoor
toilet, lighting my way with a kerosene lantern. I set the
lantern on the dirt floor in front of me, pulled up my nightie,
and sat down. UUUUUP! Up! Up! I had just placed my
bare behind directly on an unseen stream of driver ants
going over the toilet seat! Now, they had scattered and were
running everywhere. Leaving the lantern there, I ran out
into the darkness, screaming.

Driver ants were now out there, too. Our cook Mapiya heard
my screams and came running out of his hut. Realizing I
was at the toilet, he could not properly come to help me.
John came out of our hut, but I had taken the lantern, so he
had no light. The truth is, there was nothing anyone could
do to help me. Finally, I got away from the ants and
gradually got them off me. I never sat down anywhere again
without first checking it out first.

Learning to change what we can

Before I went to Congo, I had mentally prepared myself to
accept inconvenience and discomfort. Our family had
purposely decided to focus our mind on the purpose for
which we were there and the end result of our labors. That
made it much easier to accept most inconveniences. Most of
these experiences we were able to laugh off. "That'll make a
great newsletter," we'd say.

There was one experience, however, that I found very
challenging. That came on our arrival at *Mission Garizim*
(I'll call it that for easy identification, even though it was
named that a bit later, as you'll read in another story). We

had sent funds ahead for workers to build us a simple mud hut on the hill overlooking the lake, one like the Congolese lived in. We planned for it to be ready on our arrival. We didn't want our first act to be building a nice house for ourselves, so we expected to live there while we built a training school which would serve as the base for our ministry.

When we arrived at the place where we were to develop the new mission, we were led to our hut. The problem, workers explained, was that they had heard a rumor that we were not coming, so they had stopped building our hut. The shell was there, but there were no door or window shutters. There was nothing to keep animals from coming in while we were sleeping.

Even worse, they had built the hut halfway up the hill, and had not leveled out a place for it before they built. Every step we took was uphill or down. When I walked across the room, I felt like my hip was going out of joint. Worse, there was so much slope that you literally could not keep anything on a shelf. It was all we could do to keep ourselves on the bed.

I thought I had prepared myself to accept anything for the sake of serving Christ in Congo, but this was really taxing. After a few days of grumbling to myself, I called some of the workers in. "Look," I said, "this is a dirt floor." Pointing to the high spot in the room, I asked, "Couldn't you take some of that dirt from up there and throw it to that low spot over there?"

"Oh, sure," they said. "We could easily do that."

"Then would you please do it?" I instructed. That was the day I learned that sometimes you accept hardship by changing the situation if you can.

CHAPTER 5
Learning to laugh at our circumstances – and ourselves!

An embarrassing bus ride

Being able to laugh at our circumstances helped ease many discomforts, too. One of my most memorable experiences of discomfort came between our first and second terms as missionaries when I was visiting Congo every summer to conduct children's ministry training seminars. I had paid a church to rent their van and was counting on that transportation to the next seminar.

Then Pastor Mawele came and told me, "We have agreed to a sacrifice." The church decided they needed the van for something else, so they had bought me a ticket on the bus. To make sure I was okay, he would travel with me. I was angry. I felt they should have consulted me before making such an arrangement. But there didn't seem to be an alternative, so I got on the bus. It was sweltering hot and crowded. Chickens and goats were on the bus besides people. When the bus stopped, women began to barter and sell from the windows. One woman did not like a batch of greens someone was trying to sell her, so she threw it back at the woman. It scattered all over the passengers in front of me, who hardly seemed to notice.

I closed my eyes and tried to block out the heat. As we were traveling, I heard someone saying, "She's throwing up." Yes, I realized that I was. Had I passed out? Fallen into a deep sleep? I had never vomited in my sleep before. A kind

Catholic nun offered me some medicine and I heard her tell someone, "She won't vomit any more." When I arrived at my destination, the front of me was covered with vomit. When I stood up I realized that I had also wet myself and the whole back of my skirt was soaked in urine.–To top it off, when I got off the bus, there was a line of church officials there who had come out to welcome me! "Lord, do I have some pride You are trying to work on?" I wondered.

The pastor's wife, seeing my dilemma, kindly whisked me off to her hut, where she provided water for washing and a chance to change my clothes in private. I will forever be grateful to that discerning woman. The training went very well, preparing children's teachers for a remote and less-reached area. I certainly wasn't laughing when I got off the bus that day, but I laughed a lot later on when I remember the look on the faces of those who had come out to meet me. They didn't have a clue whether they should go on with their reception or not, and neither were they sure they wanted to shake my hand. I can't say that I blame them!

Language bloopers

Learning the Kituba language provided many opportunities for bloopers. One day my husband John wanted to impress on a particular man that he should not do something. "Kana nge sala yo diaka, mono ta bula maboko," he said. John was sure he had said that if he did it again he might hit him. He wouldn't do that, of course, but hoped that the threat might deter him.

"Dad," our son John Henry said, "you just told him you would clap your hands."

I had my own more serious blooper after I felt I had learned the language quite well. Mosquitos were a problem, so John wanted to order screen to put on windows for staff housing. It would be purchased by Tony Souza, a businessman friend who had been very helpful to us. It was to be shipped on a barge up the Congo and then the Kasai River to the port at Dibaya, where it would later be picked up and brought by truck to the mission.

When he was placing the order, John asked me what it was called. "*Muyungulu,*" I replied without hesitation. I had always heard it called *muyungulu* in many conversations. So John ordered it and paid for the *muyungulu* plus shipping costs.

When John went to pick it up weeks later, he found they had given him several rolls of chain link fence. Investigation revealed that *muyungulu* just means any metal mesh-like thing. If we wanted muyungulu for mosquitos, we should have clarified, "*muyungulu sambu na bambembelé*" (metal mesh for mosquitoes). Those who received our order thought we wanted *muyungulu sambu na lupangu* (metal mesh for fencing). That was an expensive mistake. So, I learned to humble myself and double check with nationals, even when I felt sure I knew the meaning.

Cutting a round hole with a straight saw

Sometimes it helped just to try to see the humor in daily life. When we got back pictures of John working on the toilet seat for our outhouse at *Mission Garizim*, he said, "And there I am, trying to cut a round hole with a straight saw." Somehow the humor in the situation struck us. How had he done it? We had lots of fun showing that picture, and appreciated even more that toilet seat hole cut with a straight saw.

When the whole Sunday school ran out in the middle of the lesson

I loved teaching African children and training others to do the same. One of the funniest things happened when I was teaching Sunday school at Nkara village. I was teaching about Jesus healing a leper, so we had planned a skit. One of the Bible school students had dressed up in rags like a leper. We had provided cold cream to make leprous-looking spots over his arms and face. At the prearranged point in the Bible story, he came staggering in a side door, shouting, "*Mvindu! Mvindu!*" (Unclean! Unclean!)

Immediately the children's eyes got huge. As if on a practiced, pre-arranged signal, they ALL jumped up and ran out of the church as fast as they could. I ran after them down the street, shouting "Come back! It's only pretend. It's just a skit." Even then I persuaded only about five out of the 80 or so children to come back for the rest of the lesson. Word must have spread, however, that it was a skit. All the children came back the following week. After that, I continued to use skits a lot, but I always announced in advance what was about to happen so that the children would be prepared.

Pizza hut

One year between our first and second terms, our daughter Sharon and a friend Jack Krajnak accompanied me to take videos of our teacher training seminars in Congo. Jack's sense of humor was always lightening up the situation. One day he pointed to a typical mud hut and asked, "I wonder what kind of hut that is over there?"

"Just the same kind of mud hut they have all over this region," I replied. "Nothing special."

"No," Jack insisted. "It looks like there's a sign over there."

Biting on his bait, Sharon approached the hut and turned over the sign. "Well, what do you know?" Jack said. "It's a pizza hut."

Worms in the cake

We enjoyed playing jokes on our cook Mapiya. One day, some friends from the U.S. sent us a packet of gummy worms. Mapiya had made a banana cake for our dessert, so after he had gone back to the kitchen, we poked gummy worms into it and then began screaming.

When Mapiya came rushing in, we cried, "Eew! Look! There are worms in the cake!"

Mapiya just stood there dumbfounded for a moment and then began laughing. Shaking his head as he left, he mumbled, "You guys did that."

Chicken noodle soup—Congolese style

John and I were staying for a day or so in Idiofa. We did not have cooking facilities, so we were very thankful when Pastor Kitona Maboko's wife offered to cook for us. We were even more delighted when in a local market we found a packet of instant chicken noodle soup. We'd been eating local fare a lot, so we thought something more familiar would be a delightful treat.

John carefully instructed her how much water to add. All afternoon we looked forward to that soup. Finally, she informed us it was ready. She brought in the soup pan and carefully spooned out a couple teaspoons full of noodles, a tiny mound in the bottom of our soup bowls. She had boiled all the water out, leaving only the noodles. She must have thought we Americans were very light eaters, crazy for spending money on a packet of food that yielded only a few teaspoons of food!

We ate our tiny portion, filled up on local bread, and never again asked a Congolese unacquainted with American ways to cook for us!

Sharon cooking African style for my first teacher training seminar at Nkara

CHAPTER 6
Learning the joy of hospitality

Since my childhood home was oriented so much around work, I had never seen hospitality in action very much. Except for relatives and a few of my Dad's buddies who met occasionally in the garage to play cards, we had few visitors. As a missionary, experiencing the joy that hospitality brings to all was one of my greatest surprises and treasures.

Mennonite hospitality

It actually began during our time of preparation to become missionaries. We had some Mennonite neighbors near the farm where we lived in Fremont, IN, just before God called us to Africa. They were very hospitable, family-and people-oriented, and we had enjoyed many happy times with them in their homes. We had seen how they made us feel welcome even when we spilled a whole pitcher of gravy on the tablecloth. Our kids had enjoyed learning to pull taffy with them, and we had enjoyed games and conversation together. But we experienced our greatest lesson in hospitality when our visas did not come in time for our family's expected departure for our first term in Congo.

Packing our suitcases for a three-year term had been quite an ordeal. We had actually taken turns sitting and bouncing on them in order to squeeze the contents down enough to get them shut. (That was back when suitcases could weigh 70 lbs., and we had weighed ours so that we were sure to take advantage of every single ounce.) When our visas did not arrive on time, we faced the prospect of having to go through that ordeal again. Plus, everything essential for living had been packed. Hearing of our predicament, one of our neighbors invited us to stay with them. So that we need not unpack, they offered a simple Mennonite style dress—a loose one since I was several sizes larger than the neighbor's wife.

We stayed with Lynn and Eileen Eicher for several days until our visas arrived. They treated us like royal guests. I am not a late riser, but when I got up every morning, Eileen had already prepared a large batch of homemade cinnamon rolls and was finishing milking cows down at the barn. Their hospitality met a real need, and they succeeded in somehow convincing us that the privilege was theirs to participate in our ministry in this way.

A cold glass of lemonade

In Congo, we experienced hospitality from missionaries and Congolese alike. I remember once when we had arrived in Kinshasa after a two-day trek on the road in the open back of a five-ton army truck formerly used by NATO. We were covered with the normal grime of the road, but were especially filthy because we had followed behind some other big trucks spewing out black soot from their exhaust. I was hot and sweaty, filthy and disheveled, sitting on a step at *Centre d'Acceuil Protestant* (Protestant guest house), waiting for John to find out if there was room for us to stay there. A missionary I had never met saw me. She stopped and looked at me, undoubtedly realizing that I had just come into the city from the interior. "Would you like a cold lemonade?" she asked.

Would I like a cold lemonade? Nothing in the entire universe sounded better at that moment. She invited me into her apartment and asked if I would like to wash up. Oh, what a treat it was just to wash my face, arms, and hands. Soap seemed like such a luxury. I was even able to comb my wild hair that had been blown in every direction for two days nonstop. The lemonade was so refreshing and I remember noting how simple gestures of kindness can be so refreshing.

A grass mattress and a leaky roof

The Congolese were also an innately hospitable people. I remember one night when we had been on the road a long time. It was very late, and it was raining. We stopped at some small village. There were no hotels for hundreds of miles around, and it would be hard to put up our tent in the rain. An unknown couple came out of their hut and talked to John. Realizing our predicament, they invited us to spend the night in their home. It was a simple mud hut with a thatch roof. There were almost no furnishings. In the living room there were a few sacks of corn stacked in a corner and a couple of straight-backed wooden chairs.

The couple insisted that we take their bed. It was a double bed that nearly filled the room, with a lumpy, grass-filled mattress on a platform made of sturdy sticks lashed together with that durable vine called *nkodi*. The roof leaked and rain slowly dripped on us all night, but we were much drier than we would have been outside. We were especially humbled because the couple, having no other bed, slept all night in the straight chairs, all to give comfort to a missionary couple they had just met. Congolese hospitality was often sacrificial like that.

Thanksgiving stew

I don't feel that we ever learned to extend hospitality to the point that we received it from others. However, we did grow in that respect. One Thanksgiving when we were living in our mud hut at *Mission Garizim*, we decided to invite some Peace Corps volunteers from the area over for American Thanksgiving.

We had no access to turkey, and the local chickens were so scrawny that it would have taken twenty to serve anything approximating an American Thanksgiving dinner to even one person. We decided to make stew out of some canned beef chunks we had shipped from the U.S. When we laid out dinner for our visitor Christine Chapman, we began apologizing that we did not have anything like turkey. "Oh, don't apologize," Christine answered. "This is the best meal I have eaten in a long time."

CHAPTER 7
Learning how much we take for granted

Mama, the kids never come when I teach

Our vision was to train teachers for children's ministries. Although Sunday school is an "old" idea in the U.S., it was new and exciting to the children of the interior villages of Congo. I had trained Sunday school teachers for a certain area, and they were eager to get started. But when I visited one of them a month or so later, he was despondent.

"Mama, the children love to come when you teach, but they won't come when I teach," he said. Knowing that most of our teachers were finding eager crowds of children, I asked him what he had been teaching.

"Just what you gave us," he lamented.

"OK, show me what you have taught so far," I responded.

The teacher opened the book of Bible lessons to the Table of Contents. That was what he taught the first week. Then he showed me the Letter to the Teacher that followed, explaining how to use the book and teach the lessons. That was what he taught the second week.

The third week no one came back.

That is when I learned that we take for granted that teachers know what a Table of Contents is, and a Letter of Introduction to the Teacher. The training I had given had not included that. In Congo, I learned that we can take absolutely nothing for granted. The teacher the children did not want to hear was an intelligent man who was respected in his village and held a position of authority in his church, but I was introducing new concepts of which he had no previous knowledge. I learned to begin at zero, assuming nothing. If I found that some concepts were easily understood, I could always move on quickly. If not, at least I could save children from being subjected to lessons on the Table of Contents.

We should have asked more questions

When we were living at Nkara our first term, we missed hearing from home. There was no e-mail, and no cell phones—only six public phone booths in the big post office at Kinshasa, so letters were treasured greatly. Mission Aviation Fellowship (MAF) delivered mail to us and the other missionaries in the interior. We had not received any mail for a while, and we were feeling a little lonely. So, we called MAF and asked if there was any mail for us. When they replied that there was, we felt it would be worth paying for a flight to have it delivered. We were sure letters would pick up our spirits. But when the flight came, there was only one letter, and it was for our daughter Sharon! So, we learned that we should ask more questions and not take so much for granted.

God Uses Crooked Sticks

John with $165 in Congolese money—
the price of a week's vacation for the family at the ocean.
And this was BEFORE the devaluation!

Sharon helps me give out certificates to teachers
who completed the training seminar in Dibaya, 1987.

CHAPTER 8
Learning to really SEE

"Seeing" street children

As a missionary, I have learned that we don't always see, even when we think we do. When we lived in Congo, young children often came up to us at local markets, begging to carry our bags. Sometimes we paid them to do so if our loads became too heavy. Often, we insisted we carry our own, trying to save every *makuta* (rough equivalent of a penny) we could.

It was not until we came to Ghana in 1999 that I realized that, after the crowds at the market went home and crawled into bed, those children crawled under the rickety market booths, seeking some semblance of shelter from the night cold. They were homeless street children who actually lived at the markets.

It happened when I had been visiting a street ministry to handicapped people led by Pastor Larry Lamina of a group called Handivangelism. We had seen many street children around, begging. Pastor Alex Boamah was showing us around and asked, "Would you like to see how the street kids sleep?"

"Sure," we replied. So, at Alex's suggestion, we waited until after midnight. He picked us up at our hotel and took us to the downtown area around the train station. There, in the parking lot, we saw homeless people sleeping on the ground on pieces of cardboard and plastic bags. Some were single mothers huddled together with their children. Some were children all alone. Some were older teens. Pastor Alex explained that when it rained, they all crowded under the shelter on the train station. There was standing room only, and sometimes a child fell asleep and fell face first into the muddy water that collected around the elevated platform.

John Henry showing love & acceptance to a street kid in Ghana. The human touch means a lot to kids who are treated as untouchables.

Soon after that, ECM began a street fellowship for those children. That led to the establishment of Haven of Hope Home for Children. After gaining experience with street ministry in Ghana, we eventually took it back to Congo, where our staff, Etienne Kinzundo and his wife Mulela had outstanding results, not only ministering to kids on the street but also eventually helping many of them to be reconciled to their families or relatives and return home.

As I think back, I'm glad for all we learned about street children, but I also feel ashamed that for years we looked at street children in Congo and did not recognize what we were seeing. Street children in Ghana confided to our workers that people seldom talked to them as human beings except for "Kid, carry my bag." Ouch! In our efforts to save a dime, we had been guilty of that ourselves for so long.

Seeing children with albinism **

During our time in Congo, we also saw many albino children. It was obvious that the lack of pigment in their skin led easily to sores that never healed, skin cancer, etc. It was not until we came to Uganda years later that I realized how deeply their lives could be affected by this condition. In Uganda, stories of albino children killed by witch doctors often made headlines. My Ugandan colleagues informed me that many people believed the body parts of albino children made powerful medicine that brought good luck, so it was common to bury a hand or foot or other body part when the cement was poured for the floor of a new business.

I first began to take a second look at albino children when I was traveling with a group of short-term missionaries viewing some of the IDP (Internally Displaced People) camps. One of the group, Leanne McKitrick, noticed an albino boy who was walking about with his arm up, constantly shielding his eyes. "I wonder if my sunglasses would help that boy," Leanne wondered out loud. She asked the driver to stop, hopped out of the van, and gave her own pair of sunglasses to the boy. When he put them on, immediately his arm came down.

Thinking about her simple act of kindness, I began to realize that giving sunglasses to albino children might be something God could use to help get their attention and open their hearts to the Gospel. ECM soon began collecting sunglasses and distributing them to help albino children in a practical way and to make friendly contact with them so that we could share Jesus with them.

Lorella with albino children in Uganda. ECM partners provided hats with rims to help protect their ears from the sun.

Later another of our Ugandan workers, Sophie Akello, was investigating the needs of albino children in her home area. She found one young girl who had been confined to the house most of her life. The father had deserted the family when he saw that his daughter was albino, and after a time, as the mother experienced the rejection of the community, she too abandoned her daughter. The grandparents took pity on the child and were raising her, but they faced so much ridicule and scorn from neighbors that they stopped bringing the girl outside, leaving her to face life shut up in her room.

Then Sophie gave them the teaching I had developed, assuring them that albinism was not a curse and that albino children could live fairly normal lives. As a result, they finally agreed to bring their daughter outside for the first time in years. ECM now has an active program to help albino children in all our base countries—DR Congo, Ghana, and Uganda.

As I researched and wrote the teaching on albinism that is used in ECM's ministry, I was thrilled to have a small part in these children's lives, helping them to be better understood and accepted, and sharing with them God's unconditional love for them. I also was ashamed that for so many years I looked at albino children with such a hard heart, seeing at least part of their problem, but not feeling their pain, and not sensing that I was able to do something to help them. I am thankful that God finally opened my eyes to really see albino children.

When the cook almost got fired

When we lived in Congo at Nkara, we bought cases of Coke for special treats. The bottles were kept in a storeroom that had access only through our bedroom. Our Congolese cook Mapiya was not supposed to be in either room. While he cleaned certain areas of the house, we took responsibility for cleaning these ourselves. This gave us some privacy, and besides, it was culturally unacceptable to enter someone else's bedroom.

God Uses Crooked Sticks

That's why we were surprised that Coke kept coming up missing. Every family member swore that they had not touched the Coke, and our adopted daughter Kristi did not even walk yet. We all believed it must be our cook Mapiya who was stealing our Coke while we were at the Bible school teaching or maybe down at the lake swimming. We discussed firing him, but we had no hard evidence that he was the thief.

One day I was sitting at my desk in the bedroom, preparing a Bible lesson. Our daughter Kristi came crawling in, crawled into the storeroom, opened a bottle of Coke, drank the whole thing and replaced the bottle! (Kristi was almost three years old but did not walk or even stand because she had experienced early malnutrition.) When John came in, I told him that the mystery of the disappearing Coke had been solved. Mapiya was not the culprit. Kristi had been drinking the Coke. She did not yet talk, so she could not respond when we asked if anyone had been drinking it. We felt ashamed that we had almost fired Mapiya for something he had not done. We realized we had not been seeing the whole picture.

John Henry gives Kristi a piggyback ride in front of our home at Nkara.

CHAPTER 9
Learning to see through native eyes

When the cook almost got fired—again!

Another time we realized that Mapiya really had been stealing. Dog food was very expensive and hard to get, so we fed our guard dog rice with a can of sardines in tomato sauce added for vitamins and protein. We began to notice that the dog rice looked red, but had no sardine in it, and we figured out that Mapiya had been putting a little red palm oil on the rice and taking the sardines home to feed his children.

We discussed what we should do. Mapiya was a very valuable worker, and it would be hard to replace him. He often went with us when we traveled. Taking only a barrel lid with us, he would find three or four stones or mud bricks to set it on, build a fire under it, and have a meal prepared within 30 minutes using either American or Congolese food. We liked Mapiya and enjoyed joking with him. Finally, my husband John asked the clincher question. "If you were in Mapiya's shoes, wouldn't you do the same thing?" We decided to look at it through Mapiya's point of view. He never did get fired. We started giving him one can of sardines for the dog and another for his children. When we started *Mission Garizim* years later, he walked for three days to come and work for us again.

Of course, you are rich!

It was not easy for us as Americans to look at things from the Congolese perspective. One day we were talking with a good Congolese friend. Somehow the topic of rich people came up. Our lifestyle seemed pretty simple to us. We did at that time have a cement house, but there was electricity by generator only for a few hours in the evening. Our water came from a barrel we paid natives to fill from a local spring. We flushed the toilet with a bucket of water and boiled and filtered our water for drinking. We made many of our own clothes and ate much more simply than we ever had in the States. We certainly did not feel rich, but our friend was implying that all Americans are rich.

"Do you think we are rich?" we asked.

"Yes, of course," came the quick reply.

"Why?" we asked, incredulous.

"Well, you have a truck," he answered simply.

The truck did not really belong to us. It belonged to the mission, and we had bought it for the good of the Congolese we served and used it in ways that benefited them. But—we had control of the truck, we realized. That made us rich in his eyes. Oh, how hard to see ourselves through native eyes!

Mama is in trouble down on the lake!

I love swimming and especially enjoyed living in Africa, where, both at Nkara and later at *Mission Garizim*, we lived on a lake. I always went swimming about 4 p.m., as well as some other times. It was a wonderful way to cool off after a hot, sticky day. We attracted far fewer mosquitoes when we were fresh and clean than we did when we were sweaty. We all just took a bar of soap and sometimes a bottle of shampoo down with us and bathed in the lake while we enjoyed a swim.

One day when we lived at Nkara, the Bible school students looked down the hill to the lake and noticed me floating on my back. They weren't familiar with the concept of floating, so they assumed I was in the process of drowning. "Look! Mama is in trouble! Let's go down quick and rescue her!" they began yelling. John had a hard time convincing them that I was just floating and enjoyed doing that. Finally, he persuaded them that I did not need to be rescued. But from the native viewpoint, why would anyone do something as silly as floating in a lake?

What do you do with a crayon?

Our daughter Carrie had an experience that showed how differently natives might look at things than we do, just based on our life experiences. We decided to do something with the children of Nkara that was more intensive than Sunday school and would give a concentrated opportunity for them to understand the Gospel. We decided on a week-long Vacation Bible School. Our daughters Carrie and Sharon expressed a desire to participate. Carrie carefully planned craft activities that helped the children continue to think about the Bible lesson. Part of what she planned involved coloring. Crayons were not available locally, but we had plenty for the children to share.

When Carrie gave the children the crayons, they stared at them blankly. They picked them up and examined them curiously. They looked around to see what others were doing with them. No one was doing anything. They were just sitting there looking at the crayons, turning them around in their hands. Then Carrie realized these children had never seen crayons before, never done coloring before. They had no idea what the crayons were for. She had to show them how those sticks could make colored marks on paper, and how by moving it back and forth, they could color in an entire area.

We all laughed together as we tried to imagine the children telling their parents about what they had done in VBS that day with the strange sticks that made color.

Shrine slaves through the eyes of a native

If you were to drive through the Volta Region of Ghana, you might notice beautiful birds, especially the red ones and the bright yellow ones, fluttering up from the tall grasslands. You might appreciate the breezes that blow northward most of the year off the Gulf of Guinea, or the peaceful flow of the Volta River. You might like seeing the rice fields, with boys sitting atop makeshift bamboo huts on stilts to guard the fields from birds who would eat the seed. You might enjoy the many shallow lagoons of the area where fishers drag nets and set traps, or the salt flats where sea salt is gathered in the dry season and stacked in cone-shaped covered piles to await buyers. You might be impressed by swaying palms, beautiful beaches, colorful bougainvillea or interesting sculptures of bygone chiefs.

You might enjoy the peacocks roaming freely around one of the area's popular resorts, or a visit to an ostrich farm. If you like history, you might visit the Prenzenstein Castle at Keta from which the Danish once shipped slaves across the Atlantic. You would probably never guess that not far off the main road, slavery still exists.

God Uses Crooked Sticks

I was unaware of this until one day when I was doing a Children's Ministry Training conference. During a break time, Stephen Awudi Gadry walked up to my husband John and me and handed us T-shirts saying something like "Stop *Trokosi* Now." "What's *trokosi?*" we asked.

"That is a kind of slavery we have here in my country," Stephen replied. I learned that in traditional shrines where idols are worshiped, priests call on the "gods," who often tell them that in order to lift a curse or ensure some kind of good fortune, a virgin daughter of the family needs to be "atoned" to the shrine. She is kind of like a living sacrifice, serving the priest by working his fields or doing whatever chores she is assigned, and serving him sexually against her will.

I was shocked by what he told me, and went home determined to learn more. Searching the internet, I verified that what he told me was true. Later I made another special trip to Ghana specially to gather first-hand information about the practice. I talked with Christians who were seeking to end the practice, and visited a chief who had freed his slaves.

My most memorable experience was meeting Fortana (named changed for her protection). She had been taken as a *trokosi* at the tender age of 13. She said her parents had told her they were going to visit a certain place, but along the way Fortana noticed they were not going the right direction. They arrived at the shrine, and Fortana's parents left her outside while they went in to talk to the priest. Fortana overheard part of their conversation and realized to her horror that she was going to be left at the shrine.

Her parents left by another way without saying goodbye or giving her any explanation. The priest called her in. He was an old man. Fortana was told to strip in his presence. Gradually, she found out she had become a *trokosi*. She was never told why. The priest raped her that night. It was supposed to be a privilege, since his genitals had been dedicated to the "gods."

I asked her if the priest ever showed any affection to her in the course of sex. "No, never," she replied. I asked Fortana if she ever just told the priest "no."

"Oh, yes," she replied. "All of us told him that at one time or another. When I told him no, that was the first and only time I ever had any choice about anything in the shrine." At that time, two objects were laid in front of her: a whip, and a bunch of broken glass. She could take a whipping for her insolence, or she could kneel for several hours on the shards of broken glass while she held both hands in the air.

Her story contained much more heartache, but then and there I knew ECM had to do something to help these girls. That was the beginning of what became our "Initiative Against Shrine Slavery." It has been one of our most rewarding projects, and certainly one of the most challenging. Eventually God enabled us to help some of the women get free and bring them to faith in Christ, the greatest liberator. It all began when Stephen handed us T-shirts and helped us see the practice of *trokosi* through native eyes.

The liberation program continued until it appeared that all the shrines who were willing to liberate their slaves had done so. Then God brought us into contact with some former slaves who had been brought to Christ through the ministry of local churches, and as they grew in Christ, found the courage themselves to escape from the shrines. ECM changed its program in the area to focus on evangelism, trusting that as the Gospel permeates the area, the whole system of shrine slavery will eventually be broken down.

Praying until the answer came

John and I were visiting in Pastor Eric Asare's village, Dawatrim. I was very hungry and lunch was about ready when a distraught mother brought her young daughter for prayer. She was convulsing constantly. We all gathered around her and prayed earnestly. I was finished, so I sat down, but the pastors kept going and going. Our lunch was ready, but they were still praying. I kept wondering how long they were going to pray when suddenly I realized, they intended to keep on praying until their prayer was answered! They were not planning to pray today and tomorrow and every day until she was better. No, they were going to keep on praying right there around the girl, dropping everything else until the answer came.

After they had prayed for quite a while with no change in the girl, they stopped briefly, as if pondering what to do. Then one of them began addressing a demon. "You demon that is shaking her like that, you stop that right now in the name of Jesus." The shaking stopped. The girl's mother thanked them and took her away. The pastors calmly turned and asked for their (our!) long-overdue lunch. They sat down and ate as if this was an everyday occurrence. I saw the girl later playing around the village later in the day, completely fine.

This was a new concept to me. I thought praying until the answer came meant continuing to come to the Lord again and again with the same request, but with lunch in-between.

I admit that laying aside everything to pray until the answer came was something I had never even considered, and I'm not sure that I am still up to it. But through native Ghanaian eyes, it was just the logical thing to do, and how can I argue with it? It worked.

Time is a relative thing

Like most Americans, we struggled on occasion with "African time." Valuing efficiency, we are all about getting the job done in the quickest time possible. This was often tested, but one of my favorite memories about it involved a Christmas play at Nkara. On Christmas Day, the church had arranged for a gigantic play depicting the Biblical events surrounding Jesus' birth. Most of the villagers had parts to play in the big production. It started early Christmas morning. Judging by the starting time, we guessed it would be finished before breakfast. Most of it proceeded from one scene to another, until they came to the enrollment for taxes in Jerusalem. We watched as one villager after another proudly came to the table to pay their taxes. After an hour or so of watching people pay taxes, we began to become restless. After a while, it was still going on. We decided to take a break from watching the play, so we walked up the hill to our home and enjoyed a leisurely Christmas breakfast. When we were finished we said, "Let's go back down and see how the play is coming along."

When we re-entered the church, we found that we had not missed much. Villagers were still paying taxes. It seems that was the scene that allowed for everyone to have a part in the play, so it could not end until every person in the village had taken his turn at the tax collector's table. The play finally ended somewhere in the early afternoon—the longest Christmas play we had ever seen.

CHAPTER 10
Learning to trust God in times of danger

Danger from snakes

Many people have asked us if we "saw" any snakes in Africa. None of us are great snake lovers, least of all me. However, the answer, unfortunately, is yes. One day the family was sitting at the dinner table when a long snake came in from the kitchen. He came straight, as if he knew exactly what he was doing. To my right was our bedroom door, open. He made a perfect right turn just as if he had done it many times before. Scary.

The scariest, though, was when a black mamba actually tried to get in bed with us. (This is my best missionary recruiting story!) We had just taken in a baby who later became our adopted daughter. She was sleeping in a handmade cradle John had made, which was sitting beside our bed. We had just gone to bed and begun to relax. My husband John stretched out his arm and felt something touch it. At first, he thought it was one of the giant cockroaches that loved every dark corner and often came out at night. But when he looked, he saw a large snake going over his arm and under the bed. Somehow God gave him presence of mind to lie still. When it had gone under the bed, he said, "Lorella, there's a snake under the bed." I jumped out of bed. (Foolish thing to do. How did I know the snake's head was not right there by my feet?) I grabbed the baby out of the cradle and "flew" out to the other room. John grabbed a shotgun that he used for hunting and called the night guard, Tabala. At that time we used a diesel generator to provide electricity for a few hours in the evening. The generator had been shut down for the night, so Tabala brought a kerosene lantern and John grabbed the flashlight that we kept by our bed.

John told Tabala, "When you 'hit' the flashlight, I will shoot the snake." They crouched down by the bed. Tabala "hit" the flashlight. All John could see was snake. He blasted it. Fortunately, he blew off the head. The part that was left was nearly a yard long, and it had another snake inside it that it had recently eaten.

When Tabala saw it, he began to shake. "Oh, *Monsieur*," he said. "It is only the grace of God that the snake did not bite you. He is the worst one there is." We discovered that it was a black mamba. According to our snake identification book, it injects enough venom to kill eleven men.

We noticed some snake "innards" on the wall and got some water out of our fifty-gallon water reserve barrel to clean it up. Then we noticed some more, and some more. I said to John, "Maybe you should turn the generator on so we can see what we've really got here." When he did so, we found a ring of snake going up one wall, across the ceiling and down the other wall. We had a lot of cleaning up to do, and our bedroom smelled like a butcher shop for a week.

We wouldn't want to go through that experience again, but as we look back on it, we realize that God kept us safe. We realized that we could count on Him to do so until His perfect time to call us home, or until our suffering would serve a greater purpose in His eternal plan. Another African friend came and said, "*Mama na ngaiï!*" in this context roughly meaning "Oh dear! I hope you are not going to go back in that room."

"Yes, we are," we answered. "Our bed is in there. Besides, the snake is dead now."

On analysis, we found that the snake probably entered through a broken window screen. We had felt that our budget did not allow us to repair it, but we reorganized our priorities the very next day.

Danger from Sickness--Saved by an old battery in the weeds

During our first term, our son John Henry became very sick. We had already had enough experience with malaria to recognize its insidious presence. We gave John Henry the pills that normally kept the fever and achiness under control. We knew it would take him five days to recover. But John Henry's fever was out of control. When he was little, he had a very high fever, and the doctor told me at that time that we should never let a child's fever go over 103° F. John Henry's temp was registering well above that, and although conscious, he was lying inert on the bed, hardly moving. When I sponged him with water and rubbing alcohol, his temp would slip down just under 103°. As soon as I stopped, it would shoot right back up again. Of course, we were all praying, but we still were not seeing any change.

Our only vehicles were the army trucks we used to procure and transport supplies to the mission. The men had taken the trucks into Kinshasa and were not expected back for several days. Our only communication with the outside world was by short-wave radio, but the battery that serviced our radio had died, so we were completely cut off.

I began to feel that John Henry could die, so we were discussing what to do. One of the workers, Aza, offered a suggestion. He said there was an old battery lying in the weeds somewhere. Maybe if it worked, we could call the missionary hospital at Vanga and get advice or even have an MAF plane come and get John Henry.

At first, I did not even consider the idea. How long had that battery been lying out there? Twenty years? Fifty? However, no one had any other ideas, so we decided to give it a try. Aza dug the old battery out of the weeds, cleaned it off, and hooked it up to the Smiths' radio system.

We tried it, and—it worked! Dr. Dan Fountain at Vanga suggested that we double the dose of anti-malarial and that we also add an antibiotic. We did so, and the fever broke within an hour. John Henry began to stir a little in bed, and we knew he was going to get better.

We thanked the Lord, and went back to report to the doctor. The old battery no longer worked. Apparently, it had in it only enough power for that one call when we really needed it. We thought of how God had provided food through the entire time the children of Israel wandered in the wilderness, but stopped it as soon as they entered the Promised Land and ate their own crops. We realized we had experienced God's protection and provision in a time of great need.

The next day an MAF plane landed at the mission to check on John Henry, since we had not called back. By that time, he was well on his way to recovery. When I see an old junk battery now, I always think of the time God used an old junk battery with only enough power for one message to save John Henry's life.

Danger from sickness--Heart attack in the middle of Africa

My husband John has always been very active and was not, at that time, overweight. He had given up smoking soon after he came to Christ, and seemed to be strong and healthy. So, when John was sitting in front of our mud hut at *Mission Garizim* and came in to tell me he thought he was having a heart attack, it was hard for me to believe it. I told him he'd just been working too hard. I thought he must have inhaled some of the fine sawdust from the wood he had been planing to make furniture at the mission. He went to bed and I prayed for him, then rolled over to go to sleep. "No, don't go to sleep," John pleaded. So, I offered more prayers. There was nothing else to do. There was no emergency room in the country. The next morning, John felt better and went to work on the airstrip. We both almost forgot about the original incident, but several times when he had to dig the truck out of the sand on the road, he complained that his chest burned.

We had almost forgotten about the incidents. When we were in Kinshasa, a missionary doctor friend offered to give us both physicals. As Dr. Julia Weeks wrapped up John's exam she asked, "Anything else?" John remembered the chest pains and mentioned it.

"EKG. Tomorrow morning at 8 a.m." Dr. Weeks instructed. As soon as she looked at the EKG, she confirmed that John had experienced a heart attack—at least one.

John began to explain that it would be inconvenient for him to go back to the States right now. He was in the middle of building the Training Center. Couldn't he go back to the mission now and take care of his heart after the building was completed? The doctor was a missionary herself, so she understood his commitment to his work. She wanted to try a treatment she had read about that she thought could help him, but she needed to order supplies for it. She gave him permission to go back to Garizim while we were waiting for the supplies, as long as he only supervised and did not do any heavy work. John went back to the mission for about six months and supervised as the workers completed the training center. During those months, we were able to officially open both the airstrip and the African Leadership Training Center.

Back in Kinshasa, John checked in with the doctor. They laid plans to do the procedure there in Congo. We left her office and began to run other errands, but soon we saw her car behind ours on *Trente Juin*, the main avenue through downtown Kinshasa, flashing her lights. When we stopped, the doctor told us that she had got a second opinion, and that he needed to go home to the States for treatment—right away.

John tried the prescribed treatment in the U.S. He found it made his legs feel much better, but an echocardiogram still showed a major blockage in his heart. But before the results came back from the echocardiogram, he had another heart attack. The doctor did an angiogram, and John watched the screen as the dye did not go anywhere, confirming multiple major blockages, and he was scheduled for surgery the next day.

When the nurses tried to remove the shunt from the angiogram, he had another attack and was taken to surgery immediately. After recovering from quadruple bypass, we continued our work in Congo. How did he survive the heart attacks in Congo? John often quotes Dr. Jay Fernlund, one of his professors in Moody extension Bible school. "We are immortal until God's time for us on earth is completed." How thankful we are for God's grace to keep John's heart ticking while he shoveled sand in tropical weather while having a heart attack—at least one.

The tractor that wanted to go in the river

We were in the river port of Mangai to pick up a tractor and some building supplies that had come up the Congo and then the Kasai river on a barge. On arrival, we discovered that the key to the tractor had been left in Kinshasa. Our mechanic Mukwa was finally able to arc the starter with a screwdriver and get it started.

To get the tractor off the barge, we had to use two large planks about 20 to 25 feet long. John would drive it onto the planks first and then onto the shore. The planks looked strong, about three inches thick, so the plan sounded feasible. However, as soon as the weight of the tractor was fully on the planks, they immediately bowed down in a deep U shape. Now being so low, the tractor was not able to climb up the other side of the U to the bank. There was barely enough room for the width of the tires, and they quickly began to slip to the side. Several times John tried gently backing up a little to get up more steam to make the ascent. Every time the tires slipped more and more to the side, until they were only half on the planks. It was apparent that further attempts would be useless, and it looked like the tractor was going to end up in the river with John on it.

God Uses Crooked Sticks

Our son John Henry had an idea. He suggested weighting
the truck that was on shore with bags of cement and then
chaining it to the tractor for one last attempt to get the
tractor up the bank. We all knew that if this did not
succeed, the tractor would be lost and John's life at risk as
well. John Henry led our workers in filling the truck with
cement. He hitched the chain to the tractor. When John
said, "Go!" John Henry put the truck in low gear and John
tried again with the tractor. Slowly, half on and half off the
plank, the tractor climbed up the steep U shape, and on to
the shore. What shouting and rejoicing we heard, not only
from our workers, but from everyone who had gathered
around to watch the *mundele's* (white man's) tractor sink in
the Kasai River. We all knew that once again, God had
delivered us from an impossible situation by His grace.

The stream that looked shallow

Another day I had gone in the early morning to teach a Bible
lesson in a school chapel at the nearby village of Lako-
Mbulu. It was not far, but to get there I had to balance
myself on a log bridge that crossed a large stream, pick my
way on logs and stones through a marsh, and follow a path
through the forest. On the way home, I noticed another path
that looked more direct. I thought it might be faster, and I
might get home sooner for breakfast. Everything went well
until I got to the stream. I knew that when I crossed it, I
would climb a small hill and be home.

There was no crossing log there, but the stream looked
shallow. I could easily see the bottom. My sandals would
dry quickly, I knew, so I hoisted up my ankle-length skirt
and stepped in to cross the stream.

Whoom! Immediately I sank in—way up to my shoulders! The bottom that had looked so firm was not firm at all, but was a slushy mud. I threw my Bible on shore, glad I was carrying it in a plastic bag. I knew I was close to home, so I yelled. "Help! Help! I need help! I am stuck in the mud!" But no one seemed to hear.

I noticed there was a clump of weeds to my back and bare tree roots on shore in front of me, so I began pushing against the clump of weeds with my feet, and grabbing the tree roots with my hands. Gradually I was able to worm my way out of that mud hole. I was shaking. It was one of the scariest things that had happened to me. Finally, I was out, on the same side of the stream where I started, dripping with mud. My long dress made it feel especially burdensome. Then I had no choice but to retrace my steps back to the main path. When I arrived home, John was waiting breakfast for me, and there I was, still covered with mud. After that I stayed on the main forest path and never again stepped into an unknown stream.

A detour through an old palm plantation

Our first term, we had shipped sea containers from home containing supplies we thought we would need for our life and ministry in Congo. We were excited when the containers arrived at the port city of Matadi. After clearing customs, the containers were lifted on to the flat beds of the mission trucks—one Jim Smith's and one ours·· for transport to the interior. Early in the trip, we hit a bump and the containers shifted several inches to the right. This made the load a little uneven, but the containers were chained on to the trucks, so we didn't worry too much.

Things went well until we got near Kikwit. There, the road we needed to travel was closed. We were informed that we would need to work our way through an old abandoned palm plantation. The road was narrow and very uneven. Jim Smith put his motorcycle helmet on for safety, we put the trucks in low gear and crept along at the slowest possible speed. Jim led the way with his truck, and our family followed behind in ours. Over and over, we would gasp as we saw the truck begin to tip dangerously to the side as it inched over the rough, uneven path. The tires on the left side actually came off the ground as the truck tipped to the right. Then it would come down again. It was extremely nerve-wracking. Did God send His angels to push the truck back down to the road again so that it did not overturn? We didn't see any angels, but honestly, we couldn't think of any other explanation for what we were seeing. Were we ever thankful when the sea containers arrived safely at Mission Nkara! Unloading them was just like Christmas, made all the more special by the miracle we had just observed firsthand.

The office is on fire! And we are locked in!

In the years when John and I were International Co-Directors for ECM, we traveled back and forth to the countries ECM served. Sometimes we traveled individually, depending on what we planned to be doing. One year I was traveling by myself and was staying in ECM's office in Kampala, the capital of Uganda. We had outfitted one room with a sink, shower, hot plate, small apartment-sized refrigerator, and bed. I was usually quite comfortable there. I had just arrived the night before and was dirty and tired, but I knew things would seem better after a night's sleep and after I had a chance to get our supplies organized.

Early in the morning I lit the flame on the gas-powered hot plate to make myself some breakfast. Immediately, the flame jumped to the rubber hose feeding the burner. Apparently, there was a crack or something in it, and it caught on fire. I quickly turned off the burner, but the fire continued. In just a few seconds, it followed the hose all the way back to the gas cylinder. At that point, the cylinder was spewing out huge flames like a blow torch. It was under the table and the table caught on fire. I was afraid I would be burned if I tried to turn the control off on the cylinder itself. The fire seemed out of control, and I was afraid the cylinder might explode.

Our granddaughter Whitney was with me, and Angela Gast, a short-term missionary. I yelled at them to get out of the house and grabbed my purse, which contained the funds for everyone for our trip. We all ran out to the main room, but found that the front door was locked, and none of us could remember where we had put the key. It was still too dark to see well. We fumbled around in the semi-darkness, but did not find the key. Our granddaughter Whitney was jumping up and down shouting, "I just can't believe this is happening!"

I grabbed my cell phone and hit the first number I could find. It was Sophie, our treasurer for the Uganda work, and a dear sister in Christ. "The office is on fire!" I shouted. "And we are locked in!"

We got as far away from the flaming gas cylinder as we could, protecting ourselves as best we could in case it exploded. In a few minutes, Ben Byekwaso, one of ECM's project workers, opened the front door, ran into the room, and turned off the gas cylinder. Ben lived nearby, and Sophie had called him. Finding the front gate locked, Ben had scaled the wall and used his key to open the front door. What a hug I gave him, literally feeling that he had saved our lives.

Fortunately, neither the curtains nor bedding had caught fire. The table was charred and there was a huge black spot all the way up the wall. The fire had burned out the electric plug by the table and the electric wire all the way up the wall. Otherwise everything was safe. The old, defective hose from the cylinder to the burner was replaced later that day, and I safely used the hot plate for the rest of my time in Kampala. I am so thankful for the way God used Sophie and Ben to preserve both our lives and the ECM office.

Angels on the gate

Angels were actually seen on another occasion. This time we were near the end of our second term. We had been living at *Mission Garizim* and were in Kinshasa when the army mutinied. We were staying at a mission guest house run by our friends Jim and Dawn Sawatsky, who worked with the Christian and Missionary Alliance. Dawn had already fled across the Congo River to Brazzaville when new trouble broke out, and Jim Sawatsky was at the guest house with us and some of their Congolese workers. We had all been house-bound for several days because of the trouble.

Soldiers had been looting all over town, and word was out that the neighborhood where we were staying was supposed to be next. We could hear frequent gunfire. No part of the city was safe, so there was nowhere to go, no way to get out. One night, hearing gunfire close by, I got up and dressed so that if soldiers came, at least they would not find me in a night-time outfit that some of them might consider provocative.

The day came when our neighborhood was supposed to be looted. I had never felt closer to death. Realizing that this could be our last night on earth, we gathered on the front porch with the guard who was on duty and committed our lives to God. It was strange and wonderful. Tears flowed down our faces, but peace also filled our hearts. We knew we might die that night, and we knew that it was okay. We sang some hymns together, on our knees.

That night, the men insisted I sleep in the radio studio of *Sango Malamu* (Good News), which they considered the most secure building around. I woke up in a few hours fighting off soldiers who were trying to tie me up, but it was only a dream.

The next morning, we thanked God we were still alive. The soldiers had never come. As we discussed the situation, Jim Sawatsky told us that the old guard Papa Makunza told him that during the night, he had looked up and seen angels all across the front gate.

I remember Jim saying, "I'm not too much into seeing angels, and from most people, I would not believe such a report. But I'm telling you, if Papa Makunza says he saw angels, you can be sure they were there." Shortly, Jim joined Dawn in Brazzaville, and the U.S. Embassy put us and other Americans into protective custody in an apartment building, where we shared an apartment with Paul and Cindy Butler and family until the trouble blew over.

Camouflaging five tons of truck

We were at *Mission Garizim* in 1997 when we heard that the
soldiers of Laurent Kabila were only twenty miles from us as
they marched their way through the Congo, seeking to
depose Mobutu Sese Seko, Congo's dictator-president of
thirty-one years. We knew that as they moved through the
country, most missions had been stripped bare, down to
cement floors.

We were willing to stay and face danger if our presence
could help or encourage our African friends and staff.
However, as we conferred together about what to do, they
told us our presence would surely draw attention to the
mission and therefore put their lives in danger. With great
sadness but without hesitation, we called an MAF plane to
come and get us. We spent the night at the American
Baptist mission station at Vanga, and traveled to Kinshasa
the next day. We returned briefly in 1998, John to help
build staff housing and me to check on the training being
given. Later I developed skeletal issues that restricted my
mobility and my capacity to travel on deep-rutted roads that
twisted and contorted my body, so that was the last time we
were ever able to go to *Mission Garizim*.

After we left, our people hid the dispensary equipment and
other valuable items from the mission in the woods before
hiding there themselves. The big five-ton *Mission Garizim*
truck was out on evangelism when they heard the news.
They realized that they could not return to the mission, and
they knew that the sound of the truck would echo across the
hills and valleys and draw the attention of the soldiers. Our
people turned the engine off and pushed that giant of a thing
by sheer muscle power off the road and into the bush, where

they cut big pieces of brush to cover and camouflage the truck.

Much later, the truck returned to *Mission Garizim*. The soldiers did arrive at the mission, but we lost only a few manual typewriters, some barrels of diesel fuel, and all the canned meat we had brought from home—far, far less than most other groups. Our people were not harmed.

During the following year, we were unable to get funds to *Mission Garizim* or to have any communication with them. We assumed they had to close the training center, and said so in our newsletter. We later discovered that they did not do so. With no funding, but assuming that we would pay them later when we could, the training center continued, developing "teachers of teachers" for children's ministries in Congo.

Ebola terror

In 1995, John left me at *Mission Garizim* and took the five-ton mission truck to Kinshasa. David Bryant, who later became an ECM board member, was returning home after a visit to Garizim. Along the way they stopped at Kikwit, the provincial capital, and attended church on Sunday. In the service, a doctor got up and talked about a dangerous disease that was little understood and was spreading quickly. She recommended being extra careful to observe all the normal sanitary precautions—but more so than usual. John noticed that on the street, people were not shaking hands as usual. Instead they would just hold a hand in the air as greeting. This normally would have been considered very impolite in Congolese society, and John joked with others about the "Kikwit handshake." John and David stayed at the church guest house overnight and took an MAF flight the next day, our mission mechanic Mukwa following with the truck so that supplies could be brought back to Garizim.

Shortly after they all arrived in Kinshasa, the CDC was brought in to investigate the situation in Kikwit. More and more people were dying from this strange disease, and it seemed to be highly contagious. Just hours after Mukwa arrived in Kinshasa with the truck, the disease was identified as Ebola. The entire Bandundu Province was placed under quarantine and the borders were closed. A long line of trucks was stuck on the road just outside Kinshasa, unable to enter the city. I learned later that John tried to get me out to join him in Kinshasa, since we didn't know how long the quarantine would last. He could not obtain permission.

Meanwhile, I was back at *Mission Garizim*. I could hear chatter on the radio, but could not send messages out. Before the quarantine was placed, I had been hearing different missionaries advised to leave without any explanation being given. I knew something was up. Eventually I learned it was Ebola and that we were under quarantine. My first concern was food for the mission family—the students and mission workers and their families. Supplies were already short, so I instituted rations to try to stretch the supplies as long as I could. It was not popular, but sensing the danger of the situation, people cooperated.

I also pondered what I would do if Ebola broke out there at Garizim, or if an Ebola case was discovered at the mission dispensary. Fortunately, that never happened.

When the quarantine was lifted, John and Mukwa came back, and I learned more about what had happened. We realized then that John and David had slept only two hundred yards from the hospital which was the epicenter of the Ebola outbreak. We learned that two nuns who had cared for an Ebola patient had died. Then the person who cared for them died, and the next caregiver as well. In all, two hundred forty-four people had died. The danger from handling the contaminated bodies was so great that they had been pushed into a mass grave with a bulldozer. Only then did we realize the danger the men had been in and how astounding was God's protection over them.

CHAPTER 11
Learning how God provides for us

When money becomes worthless

During our second term in Congo, the currency suffered catastrophic devaluation. Hyper-inflation was said to be over 23,000%. When the "Zaire" note of currency had first been issued, one was worth $2 U.S. During our second term, million Zaire notes (the highest bill available) were worth only pennies, and that decreased so rapidly that it was impossible to keep ahead of it.

In the early stages this meant that we had to carry a huge duffel bag full of money to pay for common purchases. It was very inconvenient—heavy, easy to miscount, and all too obvious. We felt like sitting ducks waiting for thieves. One of our favorite pictures from this time is of my husband John paying for the guest house where our family took a week's vacation on the beach at Moanda. The bills are stacked up all across his chest, but it only amounted to $165. That was inconvenient, but it got a whole lot worse.

I remembered how I had criticized the Congolese for not saving money, and I realized that to save anything in such an economy was both impossible and pointless. At the height of it, if we exchanged money in Kinshasa (which was the only place we could do so), it would have lost over half its value by the time we got back to the interior.

We learned to survive by doing what everyone else did who had any money at all. As soon as we exchanged funds, we immediately invested it all by buying things we knew would sell in the interior: salt, dried fish, tomato paste, pens, student notebooks, cloth, soap. Then we would gradually sell those items at current prices, retrieving our funds. As the funds were retrieved, we were able to pay our workers and buy other items locally. The point was never to let money stay in your hands for long, because it was losing value by the hour.

The Zaire note was divided into 100 parts just like with our dollar and cents. The coins were called *makutas*. Of course, since even million-Zaire notes were practically valueless, makutas were even more so. There was nothing you could buy with makutas—not even the simplest, cheapest item. So, what did people do with them? The church offerings filled with them. Of course, the churches could do nothing with them, either. Several times we bought bags of makutas from frustrated churches for a very cheap price. At least they got something instead of nothing. We couldn't do anything with them in Congo either, but we brought them home and sold them for a dollar each when we visited churches. Grandparents liked having a simple "genuine" African item to give their grandchildren, and we retrieved our investment and put the gains back into the ministry to help more people in Congo.

Mushrooms the size of a pizza

Congo did have riches of its own kind. We never joined in the quest some undertook to look for diamonds. We enjoyed riches of a more modest sort. One of those was Congo's mushrooms. Our family always loved mushrooms, especially on pizza. Imagine our surprise when village children, after a rain, would bring us freshly-picked mushrooms from the forest—some of them the size of a pizza! We bought them at fantastic prices, and the children, having invested only a short walk into the forest, went away happy. How we enjoyed chopping those giant mushrooms to top homemade pizza or sautéing them with a little "*Blue Band*," the local brand of margarine. Yum!

Other local foods

Locally produced foods were very cheap in comparison to imported foods. Fortunately, we really liked many of them. There was a huge variety of bananas with many tastes and colors. People often brought us huge stalks with as many as sixty of them as gifts. When they all turned ripe at the same time, we learned to make banana bread, banana cookies, banana pancakes, and fruit salad with bananas. We once bought a small truckload of fresh pineapple, and ate so much of it that all of us ended up with stomach aches. There was fresh papaya (somewhat like a sweeter version of cantalope). Picked green, it could substitute for apples in many recipes if you just added a little lemon juice. There were many fruits unlike what we have in the U.S., and our favorite— mangoes. We learned to make mango pie, mango crisp, and mango sauce.

The children also brought us *mikungu* or "forest macaroni." It was a mild-flavored plant. We ate the stems, which consisted of many very thin layers curled up so that when cut, it resembled macaroni. We also liked boiled peanuts and *biteki-teki*, a green similar to spinach.

Special gift of sardines

One day a special care package arrived from my Aunt Wealtha, my dad's sister who had been like a second mother to me and my siblings Hank and Marcia as we were growing up. We eagerly opened the package, and then laughed when we saw several cans of sardines. A note explained that she thought we might like some sardines "for a special treat." We never had the heart to tell her that the only canned meat we could purchase in Congo was sardines, and they were available locally in abundance. We appreciated sardines, as we almost always took sardines on the road with us because they made a quick, nutritious meal with African bread. However, we hardly looked at them as a treat. We realized, though, that my dear aunt was thinking of us and trying to do something to help us, so we just thanked her. But we sure were grateful that no one ever sent sardines as a gift again.

Trusting God to multiply Sunday school materials

Early in our Congo ministry, I faced the need for teaching materials for the Sunday schools. I had taken my entire life's collection of teaching materials with me, and as I began to use them, I realized that in this setting, they would be used up quickly. As I struggled with this issue, God called my attention to the account of Jesus feeding the five thousand. When the disciples came to Jesus with the problem of the hungry crowd, Jesus said to them, "You give them something to eat" (Matthew 14:16). With that phrase, God impressed on me that He expected me to meet the need before me. In the Biblical account, all that anyone had was ridiculously inadequate for the need—just a small boy's lunch of five loaves and two fish. Yet when the boy freely gave Jesus all he had, Jesus multiplied it so that it became enough to feed the multitude, with basketsful left over.

I knew God was encouraging me to give all I had, meager though it was, and to use it freely to bless the children of Congo. Over the years He has multiplied that so that thousands of churches have had the teaching materials they needed.

One of the ideas God gave us was not to just give out teaching materials, but to establish libraries of teaching materials that would be used over and over again. Although this did not work so well in countries like Ghana that we entered later, it worked wonderfully in Congo. Teaching packets were often painstakingly made by hand, but once created, they were loaned out over and over again to different churches. Most of the materials lasted about twelve years in this fashion.

Always Enough

Although we never starved or dressed in rags, it would not be truthful to say that we always had what we considered enough for the ministry. Our vision was always expanding, and more often than not, it was a challenge to keep it all afloat. Especially as the number of projects grew, the list of needs was always long. I grew to hate telling the staff over and over again that there was not enough on hand for an important request to be fulfilled. I never felt that most of them believed me anyway. To them, we were the rich people, Americans with endless resources at our disposal. If I said we would fulfill their request when God provided, they took it as a promise to be fulfilled shortly, and that did not always happen. And if I did not answer their request, they often felt I was ignoring them. I was always in a quandary as to how to respond and I often felt frustrated by this. On occasion, I am sure I was not as kind or diplomatic as I should have been.

I knew that our experience was not uncommon. On one trip to Congo, I had been struggling with this when I read two missionary biographies that humbled me greatly. One was an old biography of the founding of Child Evangelism Fellowship. In it, I learned that the founder, J. Irvin Overholtzer, had run out of funds in his quest to let churches know about the new work. To keep going, he sold both his suitcase and later his overcoat—in the middle of winter! The second book was about the founding of Africa Inland Mission. In it, I learned that the early AIM missionaries had almost starved to death. I had never experienced anything even close to that. As I thought about it, I realized that both Overholtzer and the AIM missionaries kept going in spite of hardship, and that both missions are well-established today, perhaps because of their faithfulness and endurance. I was encouraged to keep going, even though I had to write more e-mails telling staff that God had not yet provided for what they thought were essential needs.

Because I had struggled a lot with this, I was very excited a few years later when I read the title and advertising blurb for a new book by missionary Heidi Baker: There Is Always Enough. I knew that Roland and Heidi Baker were founders of Iris Global and had helped hundreds of street children in Mozambique. "Aha!" I thought. "Heidi has found the key. I have got to get that book and find out how we can always have enough for our ministry." I quickly ordered the book and just as quickly read it when it came. I found out that the Bakers' "always enough" included being expelled from the place where they were helping street children and being forced to live in a field in tents with three hundred street children under their care. I had to laugh at myself when I read that. So, their "always enough" was strangely like ours. It was seldom what we thought we needed, but it was somehow always enough to keep going, and God blessed that tenacity to enable them to do amazing things.

Carrie and Kristi by the smaller mission truck. "Ministères pour Chaque Enfant" is "Every Child Ministries" in French. The words around it say, "The Church of Christ in Zaire."

CHAPTER 12
Learning how God uses
evil circumstances for good

*When shortage of funds brought the Gospel to a new
people group*

At one point at Mission Garizim, we were planning to
welcome a new class to the African Leadership Training
Center. We continually operated on a shoestring, but we
had to have some funds in order to achieve that. We were
disappointed when the expected funds did not come through.
There was no way we could open the training center until
they did.

While our staff was waiting, they discussed how they could
best use their time. They decided to go on a tour of
evangelism. If they were willing to use native
transportation, sometimes they could get by with very little
on such a tour, because the villagers along the way would
show hospitality, welcoming them into their homes and to
their tables, no matter how simple they may be.

A couple of our staff--Munguba and Kiketi--took off on
bicycles to the north. They took dugout wooden canoes up
some tributaries of the Kasai River, preaching and
witnessing at different villages along the way. As they got
into the rain forest, they came into contact with pygmies.

When they told the pygmies that God loved them, the little
people stared at one another in shock. "No one has ever
before told us that they loved us," one admitted. "We have

always felt that everyone looked down on us. Can it really be true that God loves us?"

Somehow God opened the hearts of those pygmies to respond. Several of them received Jesus as Savior, simply because our staff told them that God loved them.

As we thought about this, we realized that if the funds had come through to open the Training Center, we would have been accomplishing a good thing, training national workers; but the pygmies would not have heard the all-important message of God's love, at least, not at that time. We realized that God had taken something that was not good (the lack of funds for His work) and turned it into something great (the salvation of the pygmies).

The team even found one pygmy who had learned to read and write. He came to Christ, and later he came to the training center at Mission Garizim, training for nine months before returning to continue the Gospel work amongst his people.

Passing by villages—Teach us, too!

Our first term at Nkara, as we began the Sunday school ministry, we often found villages that assertively approached us to include them in our Bible-teaching program. Nkara, like many villages, had several branches. We began teaching in the central village, but as we passed some of the branches to get there, they began to call out to us. "Come, teach us, too." We were glad to oblige, as far as our human resources would allow. We were training Bible school students to teach Sunday school, so we assigned them some of the branches. We were all so glad to see the Sunday school ministry growing in this spontaneous manner.

In the other direction, we were also hearing cries from some villages we were passing. We began to teach in one of those villages, and the response was so great that we had to meet outside the church. The tiny church hut was only designed for about fifteen people, and we were pushing one hundred with the Sunday school. We hoped that meeting outside, in front of the church, would help people to associate the Sunday school with the church itself.

We were so thrilled with the response that we were really surprised when some of the pastors from our main church group began to complain. We shouldn't go to that village, they said. That church didn't belong to their church association.

"Is their doctrine different from ours?" we asked, trying to act as if we didn't know.

"Well, no," the pastors admitted. "They believe the same things we do, but they belong to a different group."

It was hard for us to understand why they wanted their missionaries to ignore a village that was pleading for Bible teaching and responding in a big way. Just because they belonged to a different group? We kept on going to that village, and the pastors of our own group kept on complaining.

That experience was one of many factors that led us, at the end of our first term, to start Every Child Ministries. As an independent mission organization, ECM was able to help any church group that sought our help and agreed with our Bible-centered teaching. So, God used the narrowness of those pastors' thinking to encourage us to launch a new ministry. We remained friends with that church group and continued to help them, but we were no longer creating problems when God led us to also help others.

The baby who wanted to die

One of the ministries at the Nkara station included a medical dispensary. John helped a lot in procuring supplies, building a special table to aid the nurse in delivering babies, and responding to emergency situations. Carrie and Sharon also helped there. One day the Congolese nurse, Mary, came to us and asked us to take a baby in for a few days. *Kikula Somo*, about two years old, had been brought in by her uncle. She was severely malnourished and had bronchitis. Her mother had died, and the grief-stricken father was unable even to speak. Mary felt that a little TLC would greatly increase Kikula's chances of survival.

Our girls were begging us to help, but I wasn't too sure. I was responsible for teaching our three missionary kids in the morning since the Smiths were on furlough at the time, and Bible school classes in the afternoon. I loved both and thrived on the busy schedule, but I was not at all sure I could handle all that if I also had to be up during the night with a crying baby. Carrie and Sharon assured us they would help, so we put it to a family vote. Everyone was in favor. *Kikula* was to come to our home to be loved and nursed back to health.

We were glad to help, but when *Kikula* arrived at our home, we were surprised to see that she looked more like a sickly six-month-old than a two-year-old child. Her legs and arms were very thin, and she was unable to walk or even to stand. Her stomach was distended from kwashkior, a condition when the body begins to eat itself as a result of severe and prolonged protein deficiency. Another sign of that malnutrition was her shaved head, with the tiniest bits of orange hair showing at the roots. Otherwise, her body was thin and weak, with little muscle. We questioned whether she was really two years old, but the nurse informed us that in developing countries, they estimate a child's age from their teeth, and *Kikula* had a full set of teeth. We found out years later that she was actually six months older than that.

We didn't have any special baby equipment, but we made her a little bed in a cardboard box. In fact, *Kikula* did not cry much in the night, and the girls were a wonderful help with her other care.

She was not accustomed to our food, but she liked pancakes, and we found that if we put other food on top of a pancake, she would always eat it. She also loved bananas. It was amazing to watch her eat one. It looked like pushing it into a food grinder, it went down so fast. In addition to milk, she ate ravenously. The only trouble was, she could not keep food down. We soon learned we needed to move her high chair away from the dining table, since for weeks she vomited every meal soon after eating it. She must have retained some of the nutrition, however, because she began to gain strength. Soon she was gaining weight and the bronchitis was gone.

Every time one of us would walk by *Kikula*, we would try to pull her to her feet. She always cried out in pain. It was several months before she finally gained the strength to stand and then to walk.

Now that *Kikula* was better, it was time to return her to her family. We talked to the nurse about calling the uncle to come and get her. But as we considered it, we realized that her condition was likely to deteriorate again in the village. Her mother was dead, and her father incapacitated. "Can't we keep her?" our kids all asked. "Can't we adopt her?"

Adoption, even inter-racial or inter-cultural adoption, was something we actually had considered in the past, so it was not a completely foreign idea. In fact, we liked it. Our kids were enjoying having *Kikula* around. What would it look like if she joined our family?

When we suggested the idea to the uncles, they seemed relieved. I think they realized they did not have the capacity to care for her. They readily agreed, and so did the father. We had an agreement drawn up in the village language. We signed it, all *Kikula's* relatives signed with their thumbprints, and witnesses signed, too.

Then we took the agreement to Bulungu, the local government seat. All *Kikula's* relatives were called in to court. A judge asked them about their ability to care for Kikula. One by one, they said they were unable, and asked the judge to let us take her. It took about six trips to the government seat, a good long day's drive, to get all the relatives there so that the judge was satisfied that there was no relative who could care for her and that letting us adopt her was in *Kikula's* best interest. It helped that she was already living with us and had adapted well to our home.

A very long, multi-paged document was drawn up in French, and Kikula became our daughter. We gave her the American name Kristianne and kept her African name, Kikula Somo, as her middle name. We figured that if she lived in America, she could use her American name, or if she lived in Africa or just preferred to emphasize her African heritage, she could use her African name. When we later came to the States, both the tribal document and the long French document we got at Bulungu had to be translated into English in order for Kristi to get a visa.

Later, when we returned to the States, a lawyer friend found a sympathetic judge and explained our situation. He said, "The U.S. recognizes foreign adoptions, so I can just review and ratify the papers." He did not even charge us, so the six trips to Bulungu turned out to be our biggest expense in adopting Kristi. She was given a delayed Indiana birth certificate at that time and later naturalized as an American citizen.

After some time with us, Kristi went back from America for a visit to her village. We knew it was a big occasion when they got out horns made from elephant tusks, and blew them repeatedly in a five-note succession of traditional music. These instruments had been passed down from their ancestors. They were carefully guarded and brought out only on very special occasions. There was a long dance in a big circle, and we participated. Everyone was amazed when they saw how well Kristi looked. "The baby who wanted to die has come home," they all said, shaking their heads in amazement.

So, God used a tough time at the beginning of Kristi's life to bring blessing to her and to our family as well.

Another baby joins our family

Kristi grew into a lovely teenager and was with us when we were starting Mission Garizim our second term. A young couple, Erik and Bambi Carlson, were with us for a year, and Erik helped homeschool Kristi, amongst several other duties. Kristi loved to spend time visiting the local families, and it was reported that she "talked their arms off."

When we were preparing to come home at the end of that term, Kristi kept getting sick. We thought at first that she must have malaria, a common sickness we all struggled with on a more-or-less regular basis. Then we thought she might have a parasite. She wanted to sleep all the time and seemed to have no energy. Her stomach also seemed constantly upset. She basically slept all the way home, and this strange set of symptoms persisted after we arrived in the States.

We were spending a few days with my brother, Hank Miller, Jr., and his wife Mary, at their farm in Michigan, and we were staying in a small camper at their home. One night I laid my hand on John's shoulder and said, "John, I hope you

won't be offended for me asking this, but…do you think
there's any possibility Kristi could be pregnant?" She had
never had a special boyfriend that we knew of, but I couldn't
think of any reason for her strange set of complaints and
behavior.

"Oh, no!" John replied. "I've been thinking the same thing,
but I've been trying to put the thought out of my mind." We
both looked at each other, and in that moment, we knew.
Nothing more was said.

As soon as we could, we took her to a local women's clinic,
and the test was positive. Kristi was only fifteen. This was
not what we had dreamed of for our daughter. Kristi finally
admitted that the father was a boy in Congo. He had little
education and no means of supporting her, so marriage was
not an option.

We were very thankful that Kristi did not for a moment
consider an abortion. Neither was she able to raise the child
herself. For a while we encouraged her to consider placing
her baby for adoption. We knew there were many loving
Christian families who most desperately wanted a child and
would welcome the baby.

As the time for the birth drew near, we were planning on
having a special service before placing the baby for adoption,
to dedicate the baby to God. One day I went shopping to
pick out a pretty white outfit for the ceremony. I was
standing at the baby counter in Wal-Mart when God spoke
to me.

God Uses Crooked Sticks

"Could you give up one of your children?" The question was so loud that I almost thought someone was standing there talking to me.

"No," I thought. "Never."

"Then how do you expect Kristi to do it?"

Suddenly tears starting streaming down my face. I knew what we needed to do. We were going to help Kristi raise that baby. I threw down the outfit I had been looking at, and tried to find my way out of the store as quickly as I could. I kept bumping into counters because my eyes were so filled with tears.

Somehow, I got home, sat down on the davenport, and really began to sob. John came in and sat down beside me. "You're crying about Kristi and the baby," he said.

I nodded my head. I was too choked up to say anything in response.

"OK, I think it's time to tell you this," he said. "God has been speaking to me that we should help Kristi raise that baby. I haven't said anything because I didn't want to put any pressure on you." Again, we looked at each other, and there was perfect agreement without saying a word. I fell into John's arms and we sobbed together, this time for relief and joy.

A beautiful baby girl was born, and Kristi named her Whitney Nlemvo. *Nlemvo* means "grace" in Kristi's native Kituba language. Whitney has known from the beginning that Kristi is her birth mom and we are her grandparents, but she has always called us mom and dad. She has grown to be a beautiful young woman and has brought great joy into our lives. As it worked out, Whitney has lived most of her life with us (she and her mother both lived with us for a while). Now, in my 70's, we are not experiencing empty-nest syndrome like some of our friends. Whitney is a prize runner and we enjoy her track meets, although John gets to more of them than I do. She is very social and makes friends wherever she goes. We can't wait to see what God has ahead for Whitney.

Kristi and Whitney in 2012

God Uses Crooked Sticks

Whitney celebrates her graduation from high school.

CHAPTER 13
Learning to cope with anger

When you're the only one left who has any money

Ordinarily I am a very even-tempered person. I seldom get really angry, but in Africa God showed me that I can struggle with anger at times.

One of the most trying times for us was in the declining days of Mobutu's power. Congo had been through so much distress that most "*mundeles*" (whites) had left. The government was so filled with corruption that it was not paying most of its employees nor providing for the normal functions they were expected to perform.

We didn't have much. In fact, our funds were at their lowest at that time and we had to live very creatively in order to get by. But we did have some money, and it seemed that every government official was determined to get it. From early in October through the early days of January, *Mission Garizim* would "welcome" officials from every department of government, all looking for infractions they might cite so that they could charge us fines and get their *"Bonne Fête"* (Holiday gift) that would provide a nice meal and new clothing for their family's Christmas and New Year.

We fought their "infractions" hard, trying to guard our meager funds for ministry purposes. The officials were unrelenting. One insisted our *depôt* (storage shed) was a "dangerous establishment," so we would have to pay an environmental tax. I asked what was dangerous about it.

God Uses Crooked Sticks

"Someone might suffocate in there," the official said.

"No, we were very careful to design very adequate ventilation ports into it," I explained. "Come down and I'll show you. No one can suffocate in there."

It didn't matter. *Depôts* are <u>by definition</u> dangerous. The government classifies them as dangerous, so they are dangerous, and that is an infraction, and we have to pay a fine.

We wasted all day talking about that one. In the end, we paid the fine. We also paid another one because our generator potentially shook the ground, disturbing the termites.

It got so that I felt angry as soon as another of these "visitors" was announced. I knew it would be another long, tense day of defending ourselves against foolish complaints and at the end of the day our coffers would be lighter and the challenge of sustaining the ministry greater. And there was absolutely nothing I could do about it.

One day one of these officials was giving us their usual litany of offenses when John also became angry. Speaking the truth, he said, "You are just here because you want your *Bonne Fête.*" Of course, the guy was highly offended and began telling us so. Our worker Kongolo was more diplomatic than we were (maybe because he didn't have to pay the bill). He said, "Oh, Mr. John gets upset sometimes. You know the sun beats down on his bald head, and sometimes he doesn't know what he's saying. You'll have to forgive him. Let's go get something to eat, and then we'll all feel a lot better." Kongolo took the man to lunch at his hut.

Afterwards not another word was said about John's "offense" against the man.

Another day an official came complaining about our treatment of our workers. He found a long list of infractions. We don't pay all of our workers a housing allowance. "No, because we provide free housing for them and even repair their homes when needed."

It didn't matter. Even if we provide free housing, the law says we have to provide a housing allowance. Infraction one, out of a long list of similar items.

By the end of the day, he almost had me convinced that we really were terrible people trying to take advantage of our workers. I almost felt like a slavemaster.

As my husband and one of our staff walked him back to the main road to get a ride, he asked, "Do you suppose I could get a job here?"

When John reported that, the burden lifted and I was able to see it all in perspective. It was all a game to see how much the official could get for his "Bonne Fête."

During those days, one of our other missionary friends said, "You have to remember that it's all a game, and this game has only one rule. That rule is, 'You lose.'" He was right, and God used it to show me that I still need to work on my anger, trusting even these frustrating situations to Him.

CHAPTER 14
Learning to hear God's voice

Naming Mission Garizim

I plead guilty to sometimes responding too quickly to situations in what seems to be the natural, "correct" way, without taking time to seek the Lord. Sometimes this gets me into trouble, as was the case with the question of what to name the new mission we were establishing during our second term in Congo. We had built on a hill overlooking a beautiful, oval-shaped lake, locally called *Lac Nkwasanga*. We had no intentions of replacing local culture with our own American lifestyle or renaming locations with western names. So it was baffling to me why the local elders kept visiting us and insisting that the name of the location was *Nkwasanga*. The first time they visited, I assumed they were just informing us in case we did not know. We quickly agreed to their request.

We didn't often have to refer to the name of the place at that time, but whenever we did, we called it *Lac Nkwasanga*. The second time the elders came, again affirming that the name was *Nkwasanga*. Of course. The third time they came, insisting again that the name of the lake was *Nkwasanga*. We began to feel uneasy then. We had not been fighting either them or the name, so why was this such a big deal? Only then did we begin to pray about it.

We also gathered our Congolese staff to pray with us. What was going on? What was it about the name *Nkwasanga*? As we prayed together, one of the staff said, "You know, many of these places are named after the original inhabitants, and

many of those names came from the spirits they worshiped."
We all sat and looked at each other, our mouths hanging
open. Nothing more needed to be said. At that moment,
everyone in attendance knew what the problem was. The
name *Nkwasanga* was somehow connected with spirits the
ancestors of the area worshiped—evil or demonic spirits.
That's why it was such a big deal. We later learned that the
name meant literally, "person of blood."

(For those who may not share the same understandings as
us, let me explain that in Christian teaching, God is the only
One worthy of worship, so any spirit that would accept
worship could not be a good spirit.) Since apparently the
ancestors had worshiped those spirits there, it had given
them some kind of spiritual authority over the place. That's
why it was so important to the elders that we maintain the
name of the place.

Then we were confronted with a new problem. Because we
had not prayed about this from the beginning, we had fallen
into a trap. As we sat staring at the Congolese staff and
they at us, we all understood the issue. We had agreed to
keep using the name *Nkwasanga*, and normally our word
committed us to follow through on what we had promised.
But we also all realized that with the new understanding
God had given us, we could not do that. To do so would be to
continue to affirm the authority of evil spirits over the place.
Because we had not prayed about this, we found ourselves in
quite a dilemma.

After more prayer with the group, some of the staff began to
suggest a course of action. Contrary to our original

intentions, we must rename the mission. But it must not be any American or European name. The only thing that would be acceptable would be a Biblical name. Even the elders would be likely to accept that. Plus, we would not try to change the name of the lake officially. We would just name the mission we were building there and use that name. After all, the mission was a new thing, unlike the lake.

Several Biblical names were suggested, but none of them felt exactly right. Then someone suggested *Garizim* (the French spelling of Gerizim), the mountain from which Israel pronounced the blessings that would follow them for obedience to God as they entered the Promised Land. Again, there was immediate and complete agreement. Everyone just knew that was the right answer.

Even though the elders had been insistent on the Nkwasanga name when no one was even questioning it, they accepted the name *Mission Garizim* with hardly a fuss. Maybe that was because so much prayer was behind it, as well as the complete unanimity of the African staff. Some old maps still probably call the lake *Nkwasanga*, but the name that is best known and commonly used throughout the whole area today is *Mission Garizim*.

In Africa, we pray over the most unusual things

In general, living in Africa greatly increased our prayer lives. So many things that we had taken for granted in America became serious subjects for prayer in Africa. I never heard my husband John pray about crossing a bridge in America, nor did such a thing ever occur to me. In Congo, there was a serious and obvious need to pray before crossing bridges. Often, they were made of rickety planks laid over logs. They moved, sagged, and sometimes sprang up when a vehicle crossed them, and we could never be sure how much damage termites had done, and when they might collapse.

The need for crossing grace was evident one time when we came up to a bridge near Idiofa. As another truck tried to cross, the left part of the bridge gave way, dumping the truck on its side into the river. The truck happened to be loaded with sugar made from the local sugar cane, and when it got wet, I think it had called every bee in the country. It was quite a sight we met, buzzing with zillions of bees.

We often took other precautions. Usually John would ask us all to walk across the bridge and meet him on the other side. One time, the truck was loaded with about a dozen fifty-gallon drums of diesel fuel. We did not feel the truck could make it across the bridge with that load, so John and the workers unloaded many of the barrels and rolled each of them over the bridge by hand, one by one. The mostly unloaded truck made it across (with prayer!) and they reloaded the barrels on the other side of the bridge. But the consistent thing was that we always prayed.

Going up hills was another subject for prayer, especially in the rainy season. In some places, the ground is composed of heavy clay that gets very slippery when wet. I remember going up a hill one time soon after our new truck had arrived our second term. Our son John Henry had just graduated from high school and spent nine months with us helping us get *Mission Garizim* started before he went into the army. He was driving. It had been raining and the clay was very slippery. A normal, careful speed would never have propelled us up that hill. John Henry kept the accelerator down. The truck slid from side to side, zigzagging up that hill from one side to the other, seemingly out of control but still moving forward. John Henry kept the horn blasting to warn anyone who might be coming our way, out of our sight. When we got to the top, we all knew we had experienced a minor miracle. "Whewee!" John Henry whooped. "God has given us some truck!" We had never thanked God for getting us up a hill in America, but it was not uncommon for us to do so in Congo.

Crossing a Congo bridge. The truck hood is in the foreground. Can you see why we prayed?

When my sickness helped us discover a hole in the diesel fuel tank

On one of our trips, I began feeling nauseous. Anxious to get home, I tried to bear with it, but the feeling grew until finally I asked John to stop for a bit. We were way out in the bush and there were no villages in sight. While I was walking back and forth trying to get control of my nausea, John noticed that one of the barrels of diesel fuel we were carrying was leaking quite profusely. He was able to patch the barrel temporarily.

As we later discussed it, we realized that if we had not stopped for my sickness, we would probably have lost a whole 50-gallon barrel of fuel. There are no fueling stations along the road in the interior of Congo where we lived. Since we had to buy that fuel in Kinshasa and transport the barrels four hundred sixty-five miles in order to keep our vehicles going, that would have been a big loss. After I walked around a bit, I felt better, and we arrived safely with our fuel supply intact.

The brass fitting

Shortly before we responded to God's call to Congo, a friend gave John a strange gift. John did most of the farm work himself, but he hired a friend, Paul Tatro, to help part-time with the milking. Paul also had a job at a factory where he made different kinds of fittings. One day when Paul came to work at the farm, he tossed John a brass fitting. "Made 6,000 of those babies last night," he said.

John looked at it with interest, then started to toss it back. "Naw, keep it," Paul said. So, John put it in his pocket.

Later the fitting ended up on our dresser. Several times when I dusted, I thought about throwing it out. "Better ask John first," I thought. Then I forgot about it, and the fitting stayed there. John put it in his pocket, intending to throw it out, but he didn't do so and it ended up back on the dresser. When we packed for Congo, for some reason John threw that fitting into his suitcase.

One day soon after our arrival, there was a problem with the generator that supplied a few hours of electricity in the evening to the missionary homes. Jim Smith, the missionary with whom we were working, had been trying to install a new generator with the help of Ngundu, his mechanic. He reported to John that they thought they had it installed, but they were just missing one fitting. "Just a minute," John said. He ran to the house and retrieved that brass fitting that was still bopping around.

It fit perfectly. We were all amazed as we realized what had happened. God had moved Paul to give John that fitting. He had repeatedly moved both John and me to keep it even though we had no apparent use for it. He had moved John to put it in the suitcase, and He had shown him when it was needed. Talk about hearing God's voice! That incident so reinforced my appreciation of God's working even in the ordinary decisions we make every day.

Old Pastor Mawele's response to Mama's big vision

It was 1985, and I was doing a children's ministry seminar in Kikwit, the capital of the Bandundu Province in Congo. One night I sat outside as my habit was, waiting for my room to cool off enough so that I could sleep comfortably. I was chatting with church leaders about this and that. In the course of the conversation, I shared the vision God had laid on my heart—the goal of a Sunday school in every village of the Bandundu Province. This was an area about the size of my native Michigan and my later-adopted home Indiana, combined.

Old Pastor Mawele looked at me thoughtfully. "Bandundu Province is a very big place," he said. I knew that. There were an estimated 71,000 villages in Bandundu, and at that time we had helped only sixteen of them plus the city of Kikwit with training for children's ministry. The "every village" vision was a ridiculously large goal, but one I felt keenly. Maybe I was influenced by remembering my former pastor, Bill Enslen, drawing a circle around North Sharon Bible Church on a map and telling us, "We as a church are responsible before God to reach all the people within this circle."

Then Pastor Mawele continued. "The only way you could reach every village would be to work together with all the churches," he said. "But if you could work with them, maybe it could be done." This was one of the pastors who had complained about us helping one of the churches near Nkara that was not from his group!

We didn't discuss the issue much more, but it was one of those defining moments when I saw quickly and clearly what needed to be done. When I returned to the U.S., we began working to create a mission agency that could indeed work with any church that wanted our Bible-centered approach. It was another of the ways God confirmed that we were to found Every Child Ministries. As I think back on it, I realize that sometimes God speaks through the voice of others.

Carrie, John Henry, Me, John, and Sharon on an evangelistic tour, 1982

John with a couple of his buddies from Haven of Hope at the Tenth Anniversary celebration of the children's home.

CHAPTER 15
Learning how God prepares hearts

How God prepared the magician's heart

During our years at *Mission Garizim*, our staff was (and still is!) very active in evangelism. One day they were in the town of Mangai along the south bank of the Kasai River. They were giving out Gospel literature from World Missionary Press. Our staff worker Kitambila gave a Gospel booklet to a strong-looking young man called Sanduku Thomas. He didn't know Thomas was somebody special, well-known in the area.

Thomas was a magician (not an illusionist, but someone who did magic through evil powers), and a notorious thief. In the spirit world, he had attained the high position called *marabout*, but he was feeling very unsatisfied. In fact, more and more he had been feeling that he was actually enslaved by the evil spirits that controlled his own magical powers. He longed to be free, to live a normal life. When Kitambila gave him a Gospel booklet, he immediately expressed interest, and soon he was declaring faith in Jesus Christ.

Thomas was baptized, and the staff decided he needed intensive discipleship. With our permission, he was brought to *Mission Garizim* to live for a while. We learned that he had thirty-seven demons, and he claimed that some of them could block pain. He showed us huge scars all over his back and chest. We learned that the police had put hot irons on him to make him confess to stealing (of which he admitted he was guilty). But he was able to call on some of the demons to block the pain. In frustration, the police burned him more, determined, but were never able to cause him pain.

Thomas went through a hard time after his conversion. He had been accustomed to being paid for his services as a magician, and had never worked. To realize that after conversion he needed to work to make a living was a huge shock for him. He stuck it out, though, and eventually was able to marry and have a normal family.

None of us did anything to prepare Thomas to come to Christ. We didn't give him any arguments or even any demonstrations of God's power. God had already prepared his heart, helping him to deeply feel his need. When he came into contact with the Gospel, he immediately recognized the answer for which he had been searching. Thank you, Lord, for Your work of preparing hearts!

CHAPTER 16
Learning through struggles
with God's timing

A log blocks the road

Living in Africa afforded us many opportunities to develop patience. Once when we were living at *Mission Garizim* and John Henry was living with us, we came across a log lying smack across the road. There was forest on both sides and there was no other way to get through. The men tried to budge the log, but it was immovable—the main trunk of a large tree. There was no other alternative but to cut our way through. We didn't have anything like a chain saw. We had only hand axes. John Henry and Mukwa began working on it. Eight hours later they broke through and were able with great effort to pull a big piece to the side, allowing room for the truck to pass.

What did I do during all that time? I remembered John telling about our friend Willys Braun, a missionary legend in Congo and the founder of Evangelism Resources. He told about seeing Willys waiting in a long line for some kind of lengthy protocol in Congo. Everyone else was getting angry and frustrated at the long delays, but Willys just pulled out a piece of paper and stood there, patiently writing a letter. So that's what I did. I wrote letters, and thanked God that I had a pen and paper to help me pass the time.

Sunday school waits while the kids enjoy a termite snack

Another interruption occurred when I was teaching Sunday school at *Mission Garizim*. I thought I had the attention of my class until suddenly they all jumped up and ran outside. I was confused for a few minutes, until I saw all my students jumping around the yard, grabbing termites and immediately stuffing them into their mouths. Then I understood that the termites were swarming—flying up out of the ground with wings. Congolese consider termites a great delicacy, and they love to eat them live. It was an opportunity they could not afford to miss.

I just sat there watching them enjoy themselves for a while. Then, just as suddenly as it had started, the termite swarming stopped. The kids all came back into the room where we were having Sunday school, big smiles across their faces. They sat down and we continued the lesson where we had left off.

The burden for the devastated children of northern Uganda

For years I had been reading in Christian publications about the atrocities being committed against the people and especially the children of northern Uganda by Joseph Kony and his rebel group called the LRA. I had read about children being abducted while they slept beside their parents, then forced to commit atrocities like killing members of their own family while others were forced to clap for them. Our hearts and our mission, Every Child Ministries, were totally committed to African children who were being mistreated, outcast, or marginalized. We called them "the forgotten children of Africa." As I read about what was happening to children in the Acholi regions of northern Uganda, my heart ached. I prayed for them, over and over again. Should we try to do anything to help them? What could we do? How do you even begin to help in situations like this?

No, I told myself. My husband John would never agree to anything like that. We had our hands full already, and were already struggling to find resources to meet all the needs we currently had on our hands. No, I was also sure that ECM's Board of Directors would never agree to getting involved, for basically the same reasons. And I knew that other missions were working there. Probably ECM would just be stepping on their toes. Maybe our part was just to pray for those already working there. I did that, but the burden for these children kept growing.

Then, in one week, God brought down all three of my reasons for non-involvement. It happened so fast that I could only conclude that God was working. First, I shared my concern for these children with John. I was surprised when he did not brush it off, but expressed that maybe God was leading us to help them. Wow. Later that week we met with ECM's Board of Directors, so I also shared my burden with them. They gave the same response as John. Wow.

The final blow came when we received a letter from Doug Nichols with Action International. Their group had missionaries working there, he said, but they and all other mission groups there were totally overwhelmed with the needs of the war-affected children. Would Every Child Ministries consider coming and helping out in the area? I was dumbstruck. We had never received such a letter before. Now I knew God was leading us to stretch ourselves once again to get involved on behalf of these children.

Our board approved plans to send an exploratory team to northern Uganda immediately. When we arrived, Kony had just left the area to do his dastardly deeds in neighboring countries. Uganda's long war with Kony was coming to an end, but we realized the destructive effects would take generations to repair. When we first met the children, they acted like walking zombies. All joy, indeed all emotion of any kind had been drained from them. They were unsmiling, distant and untrusting.

Slowly ECM built a work in northern Uganda, first committing ourselves to help the Tegot Atoo IDP camp, and later helping those same people when the government closed the camps and sent them all "home" to empty villages where everything, even the wells, had been totally destroyed by the war. That was once that we just rejoiced at God's timing.

Evacuation

Other times we didn't find God's timing so easy to understand. We had just got a good start at building *Mission Garizim*. Our son John Henry had been with us for nine months after his high school graduation, getting the new mission started, and had returned home to enter basic training with the Army. We had worked and planned and prayed for this for five years in the 1980's, and now, at long last, things were just getting started. We were sleeping one night in our mud hut with our adopted Congolese daughter Kristi, who was then about 11 years old. Suddenly there was an insistent knock at our door. Something must be wrong.

We got up, and there stood our mechanic Mukwa and worker Ansete. They had just returned from Nkara and brought a letter from the leaders there. It said that all the mundeles (whites) had left the country and we were to go immediately to Kikwit to get a plane out.

We were totally dumbfounded. Kristen Lund had just arrived for a short term. She was to leave now, without having a chance to do anything or even to see the work? We had not yet had time to train leaders for the African Leadership Training Center we were building. The building did not yet even have a floor in it. We <u>had</u> to leave? Now? Tonight? We knew there was unrest in the country, but at *Mission Garizim* we had felt comfortable and welcomed. Really? Tonight?

With tears flowing down our cheeks, we called Kristen and our African staff together for prayer. There was no time for instructions or laying down a plan. We entrusted one another to the Lord, hugged, and packed. The instructions said we could take one small carry-on bag per person. We threw a couple changes of clothes into small bags and got into the truck.

We had received the letter after midnight and the time was already past that we were supposed to be in Kikwit. John pushed the truck as fast as he could without stopping for a break. At one point, we heard a loud "bang," and the glass window in the back of the truck shattered all over us. We thought at first the window had been shot out, but then we realized that it had broken from the violent twisting of the road. John slowed just a bit while we ascertained that no one had been hurt, then kept going.

We knew there was an airstrip at Nkara, and it was much closer than Kikwit. So, we traveled to Nkara in the truck, then called Vanga where MAF's planes were stationed, on the "*phonique*" (radio). They said all the planes had been moved across the river to Brazzaville for safety. Then an American came on the radio speaking French. It was Dave Law, a fellow missionary. John did not understand and asked him to repeat. He did not do so, but then we heard a plane overhead. We went up the hill to the airstrip, and Dave was there. He said he had been looking for us, and there was a plane in Kikwit that we could catch. When we arrived at Kikwit, we found that the last plane had been waiting for us. French paratroopers were guarding the airstrip, their weapons drawn. We walked up a big plank into the back of a military transport plane that took us across the river to Brazzaville, where at the U.S. Embassy garage we met other missionary friends who were also being evacuated. As we took off, we looked at each other and said, "If we ever get back to Congo, we've got to work harder to train the Africans."

We were able to sign for a government loan to pay for our tickets home on a 747 plane chartered by the U.S. government. Less than 24 hours later, we arrived home, still wearing African clothes and still totally confused. At that point, we didn't really feel like God knew what He was doing.

Our home church, Hillside Community, helped us with a furnished apartment, and we filled our time reporting on our work to churches and keeping in close touch with Congo colleagues. About four months later, we, along with several other missions, decided that we could return. There was still, of course, a travel advisory out, but Mission Aviation Fellowship had assured us that they were there "for the long haul." With all our hearts, we said, "Us, too."

When we returned, we remembered our promise that we needed to work hard to prepare Congolese leaders. That became our main focus, and later events proved that it was a good lesson to have learned. Maybe even worth all the trouble of the evacuation.

Never again to live in Congo

Years later, in 1997, we were visiting *Mission Garizim*. We still hoped that after things settled down, we might once again return. We had not been at Garizim long when we received news that in a move to oust the president-dictator Mobutu, soldiers directed by Laurent Kabila were marching across the land and were only twenty miles away from *Garizim* and coming our way. If we could have been a help to our national coworkers, we would have been willing to stay in spite of the danger, but they felt that our presence would place their lives at risk by drawing attention to the mission.

Immediately we called Mission Aviation Fellowship and arranged for a flight out. Later, in the turmoil, the airstrip that our coworker Erik Carlson and John had worked so hard to build was destroyed. I developed mobility issues due to osteoarthritis so that I was no longer to able to endure the twisting and jerking over the rough roads. Sadly, we never again were able to live in Congo; and although I later returned to visit Kinshasa and Kikwit, I was never again able to go back to *Mission Garizim*.

Mission Central

Undoubtedly my greatest struggle with God's timing had to do with ECM's International Office in the U.S. We call it Mission Central because it serves as a base and hub for all of

ECM's activities.

ECM began in 1985 in the basement of our home which was then in Cedar Lake, IN. At first a desk, a small photocopier, a table with four chairs for volunteers, and some files were sufficient. But soon the mission work threatened to take over our entire home. It became increasingly difficult to live there because mission work tended to accumulate everywhere.

Especially difficult in those early days were mass mailings. We did it in-house, printing newsletters one by one on a copier that could only hold 25 sheets of paper at a time. We or volunteers loaded and reloaded it, printing first one side and then the other. When the newsletters were finally printed, folded and ready for mailing, we had to sort them. It was mostly by zip code, but not fully. The post office has complicated rules for sorting. We and our volunteers did our best to understand them, laying out letters in piles on any and all flat surfaces all over the house and collecting them into groups to be placed in trays and taken to the post office.

The first group of volunteers, who met with me weekly and sometimes twice a week, was Bonnie Faurote (who was also an early board member), Denise Elder, and Gertrude Anderson. Early on, Hildred Bertsch also volunteered with secretarial work. As I write this 30+ years later, Denise is still volunteering weekly with ECM!

In February 1988, ECM moved into a small building in Hebron, IN. I had asked for prayer for a dedicated office at a meeting of the Women's Missionary Guild at our home church in Crown Point (then First Baptist of Crown Point, now Hillside Community Church). I had not expected a fast answer to that prayer, but after the meeting, Helen Bollen came up to me and offered to close a small resale shop she ran as a hobby in Hebron. She would let us use the building rent-free. After some hesitation, we realized this was a just-right step for ECM at the time. We had not thus far had to pay for even heating or electricity. A group of volunteers cleaned it out, repainted, installed a toilet and partitioned off a small office for me, and ECM moved in. We were very thankful, but after a few years, it was evident that ECM had already outgrown the building.

Three things were especially difficult. One, we collected Sunday school materials for pictures to be reused in Congolese lessons. Boxes of these materials—many at a time—would arrive just when we thought we had the place cleaned up. We really needed and appreciated these materials, but we had inadequate space for the project. No matter how hard we worked, boxes were always stacked everywhere. Since everything was all together basically in one big room, there was no other place to put them. This made it always look and feel messy, and sometimes made it hard to find adequate work space for jobs that needed to be done. Board meetings were held in that same space, and often when it was time for a Board meeting, every available space was stacked high with boxes.

Second, there was no place to talk over the many difficult issues we faced in the growing work. We really had no secrets, but mission issues do require some understanding of background issues. It often did not feel right to discuss them in front of new volunteers just getting acquainted with the ministry. Sometimes John and I had to go outside and sit in the car in order to talk about issues.

Third, there were often several projects going on at once, all in essentially the same place, so every word spoken by everyone was heard by everyone else. We loved the way our volunteers would chat, fellowship, and develop new friendships. The problem was that often it became very difficult to concentrate on the work we needed to do, especially writing, developing budgets, etc.

These problems became evident early on, and they continued to grow. We began to look for more adequate facilities. We looked at quite a few facilities aggressively, and any time we were on the road in the area, in my mind I was always measuring buildings I saw against the needs of ECM. We began to try to save a few dollars here and there to start a fund for a more adequate Mission Central. We began to talk about it and ask our volunteers who experienced the need firsthand to give toward it. We wrote some proposals seeking grants, but found it a difficult match.

We grew really excited when we found one particular building in Merrillville, IN. It seemed like everything we were looking for. The board came out to see it and prayed together on that property. In my mind, I began to plan how we would lay it out. It seemed nearly perfect for all our needs, and compared to other properties we had seen, the price was very outstanding. We revved up our efforts to raise funds for the building. Some came in, but much more slowly than anticipated. Months went by, and the property did not sell. We took our inner circle back again to look at it. We continued planning how we would use it. Still we did not have enough to make an offer on it. I began to feel that God was holding that property for ECM. I was sure we were going to get it. By that time, working in the little building had become nearly unbearable, but it helped to keep envisioning the new property. I could not understand why it was taking so long to raise the funding, but I was sure God was going to give it to us. We were getting close to having enough to make an offer.

I was in Ghana when John called and told me that our dream property had been sold to someone else for a day care center. I can't even describe how discouraged I felt. I thought we had done everything we could, but I began to question whether that was true. Why hadn't we called everyone we knew and begged them to help? Why hadn't we taken even the last of our own savings to get it? Now we were still in the little place with not even a glimmer of light for something better. It was one of my darkest moments.

Eventually, ECM was able to buy the rest of Helen Bollen's property. Early in 1998, she returned from a trip and told us she was moving to New Mexico, giving us first option to buy her house next door. In order to do that, the board had voted to rent the house out. That made the payments on the whole place. For the next ten years, we were still operating out of the tiny, inadequate building; but gradually, ECM began to build up some equity. Back when we had considered the dream place, we had planned to sell the Hebron property and use the proceeds to help pay for the new place, which cost about $20,000 more. Now that dream was lost. I was so upset that for a long time I went out of my way to avoid even driving by that place. It just felt too painful.

We kept looking for a few more years for an adequate property, but never found another deal like the one we had lost. Eventually, in 2008, the board decided that maybe God wanted us to remain in Hebron. They voted to fix up the property and add a big volunteer room using volunteer labor. Reluctantly, we agreed. Our son John Henry was able to live with us for a while and donated a lot of work to the project, along with other volunteer workers.

It was a big job that took us much volunteer labor to complete, but we were really pleased with the results. It was a huge step up for ECM, and best of all, ECM ended up owning it debt-free. In February 2009, twenty-four years after founding ECM, at last we were in a building that actually looked like it could be an International Office. The building was much more adequate for the ministry's needs and enabled us to do much more. At last we were no longer ashamed to have people visit ECM.

Looking back, I remember one day when some Jehovah's Witnesses came into the old, little building. The sign on the front said International Headquarters of Every Child Ministries. They looked around at the one-room arrangement with boxes stacked all around the front desk and said, "So this is an International Headquarters, huh?"

Speaking with more confidence than I felt, I replied, "Yes, it is. Great things happen here." I was glad they did not pursue the conversation.

The new Mission Central, from which we still work, is not grand or rich-looking, but it is attractive and gives, I think, the impression of a warmly personal but also serious, businesslike mission. I enjoy working there, and when we struggle with storage issues, I compare them with our past struggles and I am thankful.

Even today I do not understand why God did not give us a more adequate building sooner. To me it still feels like Mission Central as we know it was a good many years late. But when these negative thoughts come to mind, I also remember how much I appreciate ECM remaining debt-free. I admit that at this point, I still can't look back and say, "Oh, that's why God did it that way. I'm so glad." But I can and do appreciate what He has given us now.

Trying to walk in faith, but still struggling

As I write this book, we are currently going through another kind of trial, and I find I am still challenged to trust God's timing. Since our original problem with visas not coming in time for our scheduled flight our first term, we have had no more serious visa problems until this year.

We sent in our visa applications and all the required papers in what we thought was good time, which included an official invitation to come to Congo from someone there, in this case, the ECM DR Congo staff. The Congo embassy e-mailed us, saying that a new requirement had been added. We needed an official paper from immigration in Congo. We quickly contacted our staff there. Then a new problem appeared. They could not get those papers without a photocopy of our passports, and they were at the Congo embassy in Washington, D.C. An embassy worker was kind enough to photocopy them and send them to our staff. They went back to immigration. Then immigration workers said that the required paper claimed our staff would take care of us, and there was nothing in their bank account, so how could they do that? We sent funds to Congo to lie in their bank account, so they could "take care of us." Finally, after several visits, they were able to get the document needed. Such papers are never cheap.

The embassy confirmed that they had then received all they needed, so we rested in that, but the day came when we had to confirm our flight, reset the date with a hefty fine, or lose the non-refundable tickets. Visas were nowhere in sight, so we reset the date.

As I write, the new date is coming up in less than a week, and still no visa. We can reset it again and pay a second fine, but Whitney is planning to go with me, and she only has until the end of the summer. Then she needs to resume her college studies.

My greatest fear is that the summer will come to an end with still no visas. Why did we ever purchase non-refundable tickets? It seemed so wise then to save a few hundred dollars. If we are unable to get visas, we will lose all our ticket money. How can we ever explain that to those who gave so generously to help us? The idea is totally unthinkable.

So, I struggle to wait patiently, to walk in faith and not fear, to trust God realizing that sometimes God allows in our lives the very things we consider worst case scenarios. Certainly, it is motivating us to constant prayer!

CHAPTER 17
Finding strength to keep going

Kids on a log

One time a dear friend, Sue Krajnak, asked me, "Lorella, what keeps you going?"

Immediately into my mind flashed a picture of Congolese kids sitting on a log pew, peering up at me as I taught a Bible lesson in one of the villages near where we lived. They were excited, eyes big, just taking in every word I said. How much is an experience like that worth? To me, to experience that even once in a lifetime is worth far more than we have expended to be missionaries. To have it as a regular part of my life—well, that's enough to keep me going. I think John feels the same.

Missionary biographies

There's no doubt that growing up in a poor home where we worked hard and found ways to make do with what we had contributed to my ability to adapt to missionary work. But as I look back, I also realize that my practice of reading missionary biographies has also contributed greatly in giving me strength to endure. I began reading them in high school when my Sunday school teacher loaned out her personal copies of <u>Through Gates of Splendor</u> and <u>The Savage My Kinsman</u>, about the martyrdom of five missionaries in Ecuador in the 1950's. I continued reading missionary biographies from then on because they were invariably interesting, exciting, and challenging. I loved reading about the fulfillment of Jesus' Great Commission through many obstacles, and much difficulty and opposition.

That practice had an unexpected benefit, too. Countless are the times that I felt discouraged in my missionary work, but because I knew the difficulties others had come through, I realized that what I was going through was nothing new or unusual. It didn't mean that I had done something wrong. It was normal, to be expected. Somehow it helped me keep my difficulties in perspective.

In my missionary career, I knew someone who grew discouraged because lumber needed for the mission work was extremely difficult to get at that time. He said, "If God was blessing this work, He could drop lumber down from heaven."

Yes, I agreed that He could. Obviously, God can do anything, but I knew that this was not the normal way God worked. I knew that all the missionaries who had laid the groundwork for the growth of the church all over the world had faced countless obstacles more serious than the lack of lumber. Sadly, my friend left missionary work, discouraged and disillusioned. I'm not better than him. I was just enabled to keep on because after reading scores or maybe hundreds of missionary biographies, I knew that difficulties were to be expected.

When John and I became International Directors for ECM, we encouraged prospective missionaries to prepare by reading the stories of others who went before them. I really feel it's the best missionary preparation one can receive.

God Uses Crooked Sticks

Kongolo leads soldiers to the Lord

While we were living at Garizim, we eventually installed
five solar panels to generate electricity for the main building
at the African Leadership Training Center. We had
classrooms there, offices, and a library. Sometimes at night
we would hook up a video to the TV and show a film for the
community. Other times we worked on the computer there.

The five panels were mounted on a metal rack that extended
out on the end of the building. One day we looked up and
were shocked to see a big hole where one of the panels had
been.

One of our precious solar panels had been stolen. We
reported it immediately to local authorities. We knew there
were no others in the area, so we figured it would be easy to
spot, but we also realized it could be far away already.

About five weeks later, a team of three soldiers came to the
mission with the thief and the solar panel. They had been
found at Dibaya Lubwe, a port city on the Kasai River,
where someone was trying to sell them. While they were
there, Pastor Kongolo, always the ardent evangelist, shared
the Gospel with them and led all three soldiers to the Lord.
The thief was later taken to Idiofa for trial.

We had felt discouraged when the panel was taken, but
when we remembered that three soldiers came to Christ
through the incident, we found new strength to keep going
in spite of those feelings.

Is this time of unrest a good time to be starting a new project?

After our first term at Nkara we lived in the States for a while. Every day I had looked forward to going back to Congo. Finally, in 1990, we went back with a plan to develop a new mission (which eventually became Garizim) on a lake I had discovered during my teacher-training travels of the 1980's. Before we could go to Garizim, we were waiting for some supplies that we had shipped to arrive. That waiting time turned out to be longer than expected. We were staying at *CAP,* the *Centre d'Acceuil Protestant* (Protestant guest house). I filled my days with home schooling our adopted daughter Kristi. My husband John and our son John Henry kept busy by volunteering their help with fix-up projects at *CAP,* and building a wagon we later used to haul supplies out to Garizim. I was thankful to be back in Congo, but the days seemed long because I was so anxious to get out to the interior and begin what I considered our real work. There was a lot of unrest in Congo at that time, and we were not at all sure if the government was going to hold together, or what might happen. In the evenings, we went for walks around Kinshasa together as a family, and the question came to me over and over, "Is this a good time to be beginning a new work?" I realized that political events could very quickly undo anything we might start.

Looking back twenty-five years later, I was so glad we did not allow those thoughts to overwhelm us and stop the work. Everything that has been done in Congo since then was built on our simple decision to look at a very shaky future and press on anyway.

God Uses Crooked Sticks

As it turns out now, things seem just as shaky in my own native land. We don't know what the future will hold, but we have to press on and do what we can while we still have opportunity.

I often think of Jesus' words. He, too, knew the time was short to accomplish His mission. He said, "I must work the works of Him that sent me, while it is day: the night is coming when no man can work" (John 9:4). I have increasingly realized that political turmoil aside, the time is always short, because our very lives are short.

Another verse that comes to mind as I think of my questions and struggles in that time is Ecclesiastes 11:4, "He who observes the wind will not sow, and he who regards the clouds will not reap." Yes, on those introspective walks, I was observing the wind too much. I needed to reflect on God's faithfulness more than the current political scene. But thank God, He graced us all to keep on anyway, and that has affected the lives of thousands of African children.

Receiving ministry through Gospel music

Whenever we got exceptionally tired, we would inevitably come down with malaria. That meant that John usually got it following his long trips in the truck to Kinshasa to procur supplies for the mission. He often stayed with the Jim and Dawn Sawatsky family at the Christian and Missionary Alliance guest house. They happened to have four VHS tapes of the Gaither Homecoming series—Homecoming, Reunion, Precious Memories, and Landmark. John played these over and over while he was recuperating from malaria, which took a week. How that Gospel music ministered to him!

Eventually, we acquired a big library of Gaither videos and CD's. I love the way the various singers do not compete but support one another as they minister together. The Gaither videos have introduced us to a broad range of styles in Gospel music, and we enjoy them all. To this day, there is nothing that ministers to John more. As I sit at my table in our living room, visualizing Bible memory verses in various languages for Congo, I glance across the room as the videos play. There's a big smile on John's face, and all his "happy lines" around his eyes are out in full display. Whenever a song particularly speaks to him, he rewinds it and plays it over and over again several times.

In 2011, we were able to go on an Alaskan cruise with the Gaithers, in anticipation of our 45th anniversary. John had always wanted to see the relatively untouched beauty of Alaska, and I enjoyed it immensely, too. There were concerts twice a day with the Gaithers and others, as well as some specials, and seeing the Gaithers in person was a special treat. They were definitely a big part of helping us find strength to keep on in times of sickness, tiredness, frustration, and discouragement.

CHAPTER 18
Finding the ultimate reward

I didn't know God at all (Mukwa)

I loved living in Africa and I loved missionary life. But the ultimate rewards have to be things that last longer than that. Ultimately, the real rewards are things that last eternally. One of those was the opportunity I had to lead people to know Jesus Christ as their personal Lord and Savior.

One of those was Mukwa, a young man who served as our mechanic for many years. I led him to Christ during his job interview. When it happens in a situation like that, I always wonder if the conversion is really genuine, or if the person made a profession of faith just in order to get hired. Years later, I asked Mukwa about that. He affirmed, "Oh, I didn't know God at all until I talked with you that day." The ultimate reward—helping one individual place his trust in Christ and find salvation for eternity.

Another I led to Christ in a similar situation was Mayele Kilele, who eventually became Director for ECM in Congo. He was a very young man when he came for an interview, seeking entrance to the Bible School at Nkara. The men were away, so the interviewing fell to me. Why someone would want to go to Bible School who did not know Christ is hard to understand, but when I asked Mayele if he was sure he would go to heaven when he died, he admitted he was not sure. Yes, he had grown up in a church and heard about Jesus, but no, he had never put his faith in Him. He did understand that Jesus had died as a payment for his sins and rose again from the dead. He had never heard that the

Bible promises eternal life to all who receive Him, trusting in Him for salvation. That day Mayele eagerly came to Christ.

Then there was still the question of whether to admit him to Bible school. Normally we did not admit new converts until their faith had been proven in a local church setting. But when I was able to discuss this with the leaders of the Bible school, we all realized that Mayele had not heard the Gospel in his local church setting and was unlikely to grow if he returned there. What better place for him to grow, we realized, than where the Word of God was being taught? So, we accepted him.

Eventually Mayele graduated from Bible School and went to Child Evangelism Fellowship's children's ministry leadership institute in Switzerland. He then worked with ECM, beginning with a salary of a meager $7 a month. He did an excellent work in his home area and later in the town of Kikwit. Eventually we needed a new director in Congo, and Mayele was named. Talk about rewards! Mayele, too, had not known God at all, but God gave me the privilege of winning him to Christ, and he went on to lead a great work in Congo.

So __that's__ why we can believe the reports!

Over the Christmas-New Year's break our first term, I sent out the students I had been teaching at *Ecole Biblique Laban*. They reported a great response to the Gospel—so much so that I was wondering—out loud—about the reports. Could they be true, or were the students "padding them up" to impress me? Maybe hoping for a better grade in my class?

As I was half-pondering, half-complaining that maybe they had exaggerated, our missionary colleague Jim Smith asked me, "Lorella, who else is doing this work?"

Right away, I began naming the students I'd sent out. "There was Tabala, Nsadisa, Matasima..."

"No, I mean who else?" he asked again, and I realized that literally no one else is attempting to reach the children, out in the interior, at least. Not in the rural villages to which we had sent the students. No wonder 1,888 children had put their trust in Jesus over that holiday break. Probably no one had ever asked them to do so before. That day I discovered the difference between a report from a place where the Gospel has long been proclaimed and a village where the children are hearing it for the first time. I have learned not to question when a whole group of children respond to an invitation. I knew the Gospel had been proclaimed clearly, and I knew that the teacher had not "led" the children to respond. It's not unusual for children hearing for the first time to respond joyfully, and in great numbers.

Sometimes 1888 and sometimes one

After one of my women's classes at Nkara, I had a chance to talk with Mama Tabala after class. (Her husband's name is Tabala. Women most frequently went by their husband's name with "Mama" in front of it.) She was not sure of her salvation. When I asked her if she was sure she would go to heaven, like 99% of the people in Congo, she said "yes." But when I asked her why she thought so, she began to stumble. Finally, she said she tried to be good.

Mama Tabala didn't read at all, so I read her Ephesians 2:8 -
9 very slowly. "For by grace are you saved through faith,
and that not of yourselves. It is the gift of God, not of works,
lest anyone should boast." I explained that salvation is not
of works. We can't be good enough to get it. The only way
we can get it is by accepting the free grace of God, by putting
our trust in what Jesus did for us on the cross. Mama
Tabala seemed to understand that. She seemed to see that
she had been trusting in works. When I explained that she
needed to take that trust she'd been putting in good works
and transfer all of it just to Jesus alone, she was eager to do
so. How gladly she prayed, telling the Lord that she was
trusting in Him now and no longer in her own good works.

Afterward, she went home and told her husband. He was
just thrilled, because it meant he would be serving God with
a Christian wife, and she would be a true partner with him
in his ministry. Sometimes the ultimate reward is a lot of
people coming to Christ and sometimes it is just one. I am
so glad that the Bible says that angels rejoice in heaven
when even one sinner repents (Luke 15:10).

Teachers who kept on long term

In my travels in later years, several times God has enabled
me to meet teachers who took my Sunday school training in
the early days, in 1983 and in 1985—the first training
seminars I did. What joy to see them proudly pull out their
diplomas and specially to hear that they are still teaching
today! It is truly rewarding to see that the investment we
made in those seminars is still producing fruit today, thirty
years later. Every time this happens, I am determined more
than ever to keep on in this ministry as long as I can.

Boys who became pastors

I was in Kikwit in the later years of our ministry when a man came up to me and said, "Mama Lorella, you probably don't remember me. I remember when you used to come to teach Sunday school at my village at Nguari-Nguari. I got excited about the Word of God in those days. Later I went to Bible school, and today I am a pastor leading a church here in this village."

Another time, much earlier in our ministry, we met Luki-Luki, a young man to whom my husband John had given a Bible during our Nkara years. We were overjoyed to hear that he had finished Bible school, got married, and was now leading a church in that same area. It was especially sweet because Luki-Luki is crippled. He uses a wheelchair now, but when we knew him, he could only crawl on his knees, using thongs on his hands for protection. I know there were many influences in his life; but I'd like to think that our simple gift of a Bible had an influence on him to enable him to see that, despite his severe handicap, he had great value in God's sight, and to plant in him a vision of what his life could become. Now he is sharing that same wonderful knowledge with others.

Several times God has given me the privilege of meeting people I had taught as children who have now become doctors, nurses, teachers, and pastors. When I meet them, I realize that the work I did truly did influence the future of Congo, and I want to do even more.

Still singing the songs

One of the things I really enjoyed was translating my favorite Gospel songs into Kituba, and in some cases composing new songs. We taught many of these songs in Sunday school, especially in the weekly training classes at Nkara and later at *Mission Garizim.* In 2013, I visited a church in Kikwit, planted by Ntima Biloko, one of the graduates of *Mission Garizim's* Bible School. As I approached the stick and thatch church, I was met by a greeting committee, singing familiar songs.

Kilumbu yai (kilumbu yai),
Nzambi me sala (Nzambi me sala),
Beto bantu (beto bantu) fweti yangalala (fweti yangalala)
Kilumbu yai Nzambi me sala, Beto bantu fweti yangalala
Kilumbu yai (kilumbu yai), Nzambi me sala!

This is the day! (This is the day)
That the Lord has made (That the Lord has made)
We will rejoice (We will rejoice)
And be glad in it (And be glad in it)
This is the day that the Lord has made,
We will rejoice and be glad in it
This is the day (This is the day)
That the Lord has made!

Did they remember that I had translated that song? Did they even know? Did they choose to sing it that day because I had translated it? As I listened through the Sunday school program, I realized that they had not chosen it specially. It was just that many of the songs I had translated or written had become a standard part of their hymnology. They had become popular. As I reflected on hearing songs I had written thirty years earlier, I felt a deep sense of satisfaction. I had done something that was satisfying for more than a day. I had done something lasting, and I felt so thankful that God had enabled me to make that kind of contribution to the church of Christ in Congo.

CHAPTER 19
This is our story. What's yours?

Dear reader,

I hope you've enjoyed reading about a bit of our story.
(There are many more stories to come.)

However, our story began long before Jesus talked to John
while he was milking cows. Our story began when each of
us personally and individually received Jesus Christ, God's
eternal Son from heaven, as our Savior and Lord. For me
that moment happened on May 12, 1961. I was finishing my
sophomore year in high school. Although I'd attended
church all my life, it meant nothing to me. Jesus Christ had
no thought in my heart or life. To me, He was just a word
we said on Sunday. In school, I had learned that evolution
could account for how things got here. I loved science and
was convinced that it held the answer to most of our
problems.

I can't explain exactly what happened to me the evening of
May 12. An acquaintance invited me to a special meeting at
her church, to help her win a Bible by bringing the most
people. I did not accept the invitation because I was
interested, but because it was so rare that anyone invited
me to do anything. I went alone and did not even sit with
the girl who invited me. But from the first moment of the
service, God began speaking to me. How could that be? I
didn't really even put much stock in the possibility of God's
existence at the time. I remember that they sang the hymn,
"Blessed Assurance; Jesus is mine." Assurance? That was a

new thought to me. Was such a thing even possible? I certainly did not have any assurance.

Then an evangelist named Billy Walker spoke. The sermon was about hell. I went in not even believing much in heaven or God or anything. I went out convinced that I was going to hell. I remembered Bible verses I had memorized in Vacation Bible School as a child. "All have sinned and fall short of the glory of God" (Romans 3:23). I never argued with that verse, but I took it very lightly. "Sure, I've sinned," I figured. "After all, nobody is perfect." But as the evangelist spoke that night, God showed me that as a sinner I was in big trouble with Him. In fact, I was His enemy and deserved hell. God could not let any sin into heaven. An invitation was given that night to come to Christ. I felt my need very keenly, but I was fighting with my lifelong shyness. My hands gripped the pews. To walk down the aisle publicly? I was terrified at the thought of anything so bold.

I was convinced that I would probably get in a wreck and go to hell before I even got home that night, but somehow, I safely made it to my bed. There, I tossed and turned, the conviction of sin heavy on my heart. I remembered from Vacation Bible School that I could call on God and ask for His salvation. "For whoever shall call on the name of the Lord shall be saved" (Romans 10:13). Finally, I called on God, desperately whispering a prayer something like this:

"Oh God, if there is a God, I know I am a sinner and deserve hell because of my sin. I do believe that Jesus died for me and rose again, or at least, I want to believe. Please come into my heart and life right now. Please forgive my sin and make me a real Christian." Something like that. Over and over. (I know now that I only needed to do it once.) I went back again to those meetings every day that week, and on Sunday I finally found courage to walk forward and publicly confess my faith in Christ. I believe I was born again from the time I uttered that very first prayer.

In no way did I become instantly perfect, nor am I so even yet, but when I called out to Jesus and asked Him to save me, it literally changed my life, even though I began my prayer with "If there is a God." Suddenly I wanted to read the Bible. I wanted to fellowship with other believers. I wanted to please God.

Had I not called on Jesus and asked Him to save me that day, I would never have been a missionary, because I would have had no message to share. Frankly, I would never even have continued with church once my father was no longer pressing me to go.

I have failed God in many ways and had to come back to Him more than once, but that experience of being born again gave me a spiritual "home" to come back to. Gradually my life began to change. As I thought more about pleasing God and less about myself, my extreme shyness began to disappear and I enjoyed being with others more. As I learned that we are all children of the same earthly parents, Adam and Eve, I began to place more value on human life, and that eventually led me all the way to the neglected children of Africa.

Dear friend, what is your story? If your story does not include coming to a personal relationship with Jesus Christ, I want to let you know that He is waiting and open to entering into that relationship with you. Just call on Him, however imperfectly, and ask Him to save you and take away your sins. If I can help you in any way in your spiritual journey, please don't hesitate to write to me.

God calls each of His children to serve Him in different places and in different ways. Yours may not include going overseas or to a different culture, but I encourage you to ask Him how you can serve Him in a way that matters for eternity. I am sure He is waiting to hear from you!

Love,

Lorella

Notes:

*Zaire or Congo?

When we went to Africa in 1981, the country where we
served was called Zaire. Along the way, it was changed to
Congo, then changed back to Zaire the very next day!
Today, once again, the country is called Congo. For sake of
clarity, we have chosen to refer to the country as Congo and
the people as Congolese regardless of what they were called
at the time period we were writing about.

The country where we served our first term is what was once
the Belgian Congo, in contrast to French Congo across the
river to the north of the Congo River. Today, "our" Congo is
officially called The Democratic Republic of Congo
(commonly referred to as DR Congo), while the former
French Congo is officially called The Republic of Congo
(commonly referred to as Congo Brazzaville).

**Children with albinism

"Children with albinism" is the politically correct term, but
in Africa they are frequently called "albinos" (pronounced al-
bee-nos), and no disrespect is intended. It is simply a
descriptive term. Since we are accustomed to this term and
it is less cumbersome than the politically correct term, we
have chosen to use it. Please! The term is in no way
intended in a derogatory manner.

EVERY CHILD MINISTRIES

For further information about Every Child Ministries:

Explore the official website at www.ecmafrica.org

Donations are much needed and deeply appreciated.
Give online or send your gift to:

Every Child Ministries
PO Box 810
Hebron, IN 46341

Enhancing Trust

Please mention that you read this book!

If you'd like to be a partner in continuing and expanding the
work the Rousters began, you can designate your gift to the
"Congo ministry." You may also support the Rousters' work
by designating your gift to "Rouster missionary account."

You may write the author personally at:

lrouster@ecmafrica.org ~~or visit her personal website at~~
~~www.lovecongo.org.~~

Ideas for children's VBS or Sunday school missions projects
are available from the author.

The author is available to speak in areas around her
hometown in Northwest Indiana, or anywhere else if the
inviting group is willing to cover travel expenses.

INDEX

Update 2021

From the author

In 2015, my hubby & became "ordinary" missionaries again, after serving as International Directors of Every Child Ministries for 17 years. At that time, John retired due to health concerns, and God gave me a new assignment.

Now I am working to make the Bible accessible and understandable to kids in Congo. It's a big book—complex, yet the main themes are simple. Profound, and life-changing.

To do this, I'm writing Bible-teaching guides for Sunday school teachers in their own local language. (I write in the Kituba (Kikongo) language, and ECM staff members translate into three other languages.)

We call it the Mwinda Project (**Mween-**duh). Mwinda means "Light" in almost all the languages of Congo, and the Bible has been described as a light on our path when things around us are dark (Psalm 119:105). It's a project under Every Child Ministries. Check it out on the web at **www.mwindaproject-ecm.com** .

Like to keep up with me more? Subscribe to my monthly news & prayer letter, _Rouster's Real Deal_. E-mail me at Lrouster@ecmafrica.org.

Besides writing the books, I raise funds to print and distribute them to Teachers' Resource Libraries we have been developing throughout western and Central Congo. From there, they are loaned to Bible-teaching churches in library fashion. Each book may be used by about 12 different churches, one after another, reaching about 960 children with the Gospel message.

To contribute, make your check out to ECM and designate "Mwinda Project." _Send to ECM, PO Box 810, Hebron, IN 46341_. THANK YOU !

Of course, your gifts are tax-deductible, and financial integrity is assured by ECM's membership in the Evangelical Council for Financial Accountability.